T0113444

Globalisation vs. Sovereignty? The European Response

The 1997 Rede Lecture and Related Speeches

∞∞∞

LEON BRITTAN

∞∞∞

The Rede Lecture given by
The Rt Hon. Sir Leon Brittan QC,
Vice-President of the European Commission,
in the Senate House, University of
Cambridge, on 20 February 1997

CAMBRIDGE
UNIVERSITY PRESS

CAMBRIDGE UNIVERSITY PRESS
Cambridge, New York, Melbourne, Madrid, Cape Town, Singapore,
São Paulo, Delhi, Dubai, Tokyo, Mexico City

Cambridge University Press
The Edinburgh Building, Cambridge CB2 8RU, UK

Published in the United States of America by Cambridge University Press, New York

www.cambridge.org
Information on this title: www.cambridge.org/9780521638845

First published 1998
Reprinted 1999

A catalogue record for this publication is available from the British Library

ISBN 978-0-521-63884-5 Paperback

Contents

ooooo

Preface

ooooo

By the time I arrived in Brussels in 1989, I had spent the best part of my adult life in active politics. Speeches are the lifeblood of politics and I had come to regard them as a normal, almost daily, exercise in the ebb and flow of political life in the United Kingdom.

When I took up my position in the European Commission, I naturally asked myself whether the work I was doing there would be of sufficient general interest and controversy to engender speeches which would appeal to a broader audience. In fact, I soon discovered that the work of the European Commission was of such interest, and the debate in the United Kingdom about its relationship with the European Union so heated, that speeches assumed an even greater importance in my work than they had before.

The evolution of the European Union, even in the decade I have been in Brussels, has been as fascinating as it has been rapid. It touches upon all of the most essential political questions of the day: to what extent and for what purpose should one seek to retain political sovereignty in an increasingly international world? What is the logic of economic integration? How can the individual feel properly involved in an increasingly complex political and economic environment? How can Europe come together to shape events all over the globe? It is these kinds of questions that I have tried to address in my speeches, most notably in the 1997 Rede Lecture at Cambridge University, which serves as the centrepiece of this publication.

I very much hope that this small collection of speeches will make a modest contribution in enhancing understanding of European affairs in the United Kingdom. Without better understanding, an enthusiastic popular commitment to Britain's

European vocation, which I have long advocated, will not be possible.

In putting this collection together, I would particularly like to thank the Vice-Chancellor of Cambridge University, Professor Alec Broers, who personally invited me to deliver the Rede Lecture; William Davies, a Senior Commissioning Editor of the Cambridge University Press; and Nicholas Clegg, the member of my Brussels team whose help in preparing the Rede Lecture and editing this collection of speeches has been crucial and indispensable.

Globalisation vs. Sovereignty? The European Response
The 1997 Rede Lecture

ooooo

Vice-Chancellor, Ladies and Gentlemen:

I am honoured and touched to be invited to give this prestigious lecture to you this evening. In 1524 the gift of the executors of Sir Robert Rede's estate of an annuity of 20 marks to the Master and Fellows of Jesus College led to the establishment of this, perhaps the oldest lectureship in Cambridge. Sir Robert Rede was Chief Justice of the Commons Pleas in the reigns of both Henry VII and Henry VIII, kings who were not unknown to remove the heads of awkward public servants. So I am not sure if *he* would have felt he had much independence to express his own ideas. Perhaps it was to make up for this that his executors insisted that the Rede lectures should 'for ever read franck and free to all manner of schollers'.

Life is much easier, on the other hand, for a European Commissioner who is duty bound to take an oath of independence: one of the least onerous vows I have ever had to observe.

I would add that I am particularly touched to be chosen to give this lecture, as the appointment is the personal prerogative of the Vice-Chancellor, and I am the first person you have had the opportunity to choose.

INTRODUCTION

Globalisation is widely viewed as one of the most powerful forces shaping the modern world. In some quarters, it is regarded with dread as a whirlwind of relentless and disruptive change which leaves governments helpless and leaves a trail of economic, social, cultural and environmental problems in its wake. In some countries, notably France and the United States, globalisation has assumed remarkable prominence in the domestic political debate. It is invoked to justify new forms of protectionism, nationalism and even a rediscovery of religious and environmental values all of which, it is said, are essential bulwarks against the unsettling effects of the new international order. This thinking can be seen, for example, in the politics of both Pat Buchanan and the French National Front, but also in the protests of environmental pressure groups and even in the exhortations of religious revivalists.

There is a further concern about the perceived effect of globalisation on confidence in national governments and democratic institutions. The feeling is that the scale and fluidity of international economic activity robs democratic institutions and representative governments of the ability to control their own economies for the benefit of their own electorates. Put simply, globalisation is felt to undermine national sovereignty. The result is likely to be a worrying degree of disaffection amongst voters, as politics and politicians are increasingly held in contempt because they are unable to deliver on the promises which they continue to make to the electorate, because the global economy is well beyond their control. The disillusionment that follows then provides fertile ground for single-issue protest movements and other forms of the political counter-culture to take root.

What I want to explore this evening is whether these concerns about the economic, social and political consequences of globalisation are justified, inevitable and bound to increase, or whether there is a response, and particularly a European response, that can and should be given to those concerns.

There is no doubt that the rapidly changing patterns of international economic relations are objectively having an impact on the meaning of government and the traditional expressions of sovereignty and political self-expression. However, I do not believe that the only responses to this need be pessimism, political indifference or a retreat into defensive and outdated certainties. Rather, we need to look beyond the boundaries of our conventional understanding of sovereignty and accept that more flexible, complex and, above all, international political arrangements need to be found to answer the economic and political demands made by an increasingly integrated international economy.

This, of course, is where the European Union comes in. I will argue that the process of European integration, whilst it had many different historical sources, should today primarily be viewed as a highly sophisticated attempt on the part of European countries to have the maximum possible influence over their future in a world of globalised economic activity. It is an alternative to the vain attempt to retain the hollow shell of total national sovereignty in a world where the purported exercise of such sovereignty is in important respects no longer effective. But integration for its own sake is not the answer. It could lead down a blind alley of over-protected, introverted and closed arrangements between governments. Rather, integration should be a catalyst for openness, dynamism and political and economic innovation.

Though it will not be easy, following such an approach will enhance our strength in an era of globalisation and enable electorates to gain the confidence necessary to adapt to the changes around them and to regain a sense of control over their own destinies.

GLOBALISATION

First, however, it is worth dwelling a little on what globalisation actually means. It has been argued that today's globalisation is a throwback to the world economy of the late nineteenth century.[1] Borders then were open to migration, total international capital flows in relation to GDP were greater than they are now, the gold standard imposed a high level of international monetary restraint and the destiny of great trading nations like the United Kingdom was entirely dependent on international trade. According to this logic, the rash of trade protectionism and monetary instability in the interwar years, and even the break-down of the Bretton Woods system in the early 1970s are, historically speaking, abberations. The rule, it is said, has always been globalisation.

However, whilst it is worth pointing out the historical importance of past international economic inter-dependence, there is something qualitatively new about the globalisation which we are now witnessing. A single world economy is being created in a way which makes the international economic regime of the late nineteenth century seem no more than an embryo of today's fully fledged globalised economy. First, direct foreign investment has become the new vehicle for trade and has expanded at a prodigious rate, far greater than the growth of total world trade. By 1993, according to the UN Conference on Trade and Development, the sales of foreign subsidiaries had reached $5.2 trillion per year or one fifth of the entire world economy. As a result, a growing proportion of total international trade, up to a third, actually takes place within transnational companies themselves. Multinationals, the traditional bogeymen of those who object to the new world economy, constitute the very fabric of today's international economic relations.

Second, the volume of international financial transactions has exploded. The daily turnover of foreign exchange markets amounts to a staggering $1,000 billion and international stock

[1] Paul Hirst and Grahame Thompson, *Globalization in Question* (Cambridge: Polity, 1996).

market transactions to around $1,500 billion. Capital has truly become footloose and fancy free, able to be transferred across the globe in a matter of seconds. It is not surprising, then, that the financial markets are sometimes regarded by governments as a direct challenge to their ability to conduct their own monetary policies. At the time of the last ERM crisis, much of the blame was laid at the door of the 'gnomes of the City of London'. It became cruelly obvious that the resources of governments can be rendered helpless in the face of a concerted and persistent movement of capital in one direction by the financial markets.

Third, services have emerged as the new lifeblood of international trade. No longer can trade be judged according to the amount of cargo stored in the holds of ships plying their wares along the great maritime corridors of the world. Trade is now measured according to the transfer of financial, legal, managerial, design and information skills. In 1970, under a third of foreign direct investment related to the export of services. Today that figure has risen to 50 per cent. In other words, it is the intellectual capital which has become the prized commodity of the world's markets. These days, what you think has become more exportable than what you make.

Finally, technological specialisation, particularly in the field of information technology, is at the heart of the innovation needed to exploit new trading opportunities. Advances in technology require an ever-increasing level of specialised knowledge. With that knowledge, the world can become your oyster. Nowadays, it is not considered surprising that computer programmers in India, linked directly to the information networks of companies in Europe and America, are employed to maintain and update networks in Paris, London or New York from the comfort of their offices in New Delhi. Nico Colchester, the late and highly respected economic journalist, spoke of this being the 'age of competence'. This, I know, has particular resonance here in Cambridge, the home of Silicon Fen, where intellectual competence and specialised knowledge have made the successful leap from university lecture theatre to business park.

Given the features of this new international economic order – driven by private foreign investment and the mobility of capital, increasingly dominated by services rather than goods, transformed by new technologies and mastered by those with brains not brawn – it is no surprise that the issues discussed in international trade negotiations have changed and continue to change significantly. The old order was dominated by negotiations on the duties and tariffs imposed by countries on each other's products. It was logical that the international agreement regulating trade should have been called the General Agreement on *Tariffs* and Trade, or GATT for short. The principal purpose of the endless rounds of trade negotiations in the post-war period was to reduce the ability of governments to slap tariffs on physical imports.

However, as the new patterns of trade emerged so new needs have become apparent. When I was working to conclude the Uruguay Trade Round in December 1993, one of the greatest achievements that we were aiming at was to launch the move towards new liberalising rules covering services such as telecommunications and financial services which are still now being finalised in detail. More recently, in Singapore last December, trade ministers from all over the world assembled and agreed to push forward the concept of international rules on trade and investment and on the application of competition policy, hitherto the exclusive province of national governments.

This shows it is no longer just a question of reducing the previously punitive charges imposed on trade, but a more complex task of ensuring that a viable and transparent set of rules is agreed which will encourage trade, and international economic activity more generally, in all its new forms to continue to grow without unfair hindrance. Alongside this much broader process of liberalisation, the GATT has now been replaced by a fully fledged institution, the World Trade Organisation, with a dispute settlement mechanism of a supranational character imposing penalties on those countries who are not willing to play by the new and increasingly complex range of rules which govern international trade.

In other words, in order to meet the challenges of globalisation the multilateral system has had to embark on a much broader based process of liberalisation than in the past, but has also had to buttress that process with an effective discipline which is *pro tanto* a diminution of unfettered national sovereignty. It is this latter factor which was one of the major reasons for the difficulty in getting the US Congress to ratify the results of the Uruguay Round.

THE EFFECTS OF GLOBALISATION

But the fact that the multilateral trading system has accommodated itself to globalisation in this way does not in itself prove that this is the only response required or that globalisation is automatically to be welcomed. Let me make my own position crystal clear from the start: I am a convinced supporter of global economic liberalisation, not only because I think new technology and reduced transport costs make it inevitable, but above all because I believe the process is conducive to continuing economic growth and therefore to greater human well-being. An open economic system is also a force for international peace and stability. It opens or isolates closed political regimes, and by either means it weakens them. Economic links foster interdependence, which in turn promotes political stability. In my view, it is not by chance that the unprecedented period of world peace since the last world war has coincided with the unprecedented growth in economic interdependence. To be sure, the horrific outbreaks in regional and ethnic conflict do not allow for any complacency, but the increasingly globalised economy and the international arrangements for handling it provide the best guarantee we have that these conflicts do not ignite into wider political and military disorder.

Nor is it the case, as is often asserted, that globalisation merely reinforces the domination of the rich and exacerbates the impoverishment of the poor. The distribution of global economic growth in recent times, with the spectacular emergence of the once underdeveloped Asian economies, demonstrates this. Indeed, the argument is often made in the traditionally richer economies that globalisation is leading to a shift of economic activity and wealth *away* from the richer world to other, poorer parts of the world. That said, there is a significant number of the least developed countries which remain economically marginalised and risk becoming more so. It is essential that these countries become fully and fairly incorporated into the world trading system; positive action and assistance are required to make this happen. In Singapore last December, Europe was at the forefront of those arguing this case. I hope we will soon take effective action ourselves to advance it.

There is also no evidence to show that globalisation can be held responsible for increased levels of unemployment, particularly amongst unskilled workers in the developed world. It is far too simplistic to say that because cars can be made more cheaply in Korea, unemployment is inevitably going to increase in the west. It is technological change rather than globalisation alone that has meant that unskilled labour has declined as a proportion of total labour in all industries. Specialised skills have become increasingly important and are necessary to exploit the opportunities of international markets. But they are not created solely by the process of globalisation. The demands of technology, which have less need of unskilled labour, are a separate if not unrelated development.

Nor is it true to say that, as has sometimes been suggested, the social security provisions of the modern welfare state are being threatened by the pressures of globalisation. There are other factors, not least demography and the rise in the number of retired pensioners as a proportion of the total population, that have given rise to the increasing strains on the welfare state.

At the same time, a legitimate concern has arisen that as economies become increasingly inter-dependent, certain basic human rights for the workforce of any country participating in the multilateral economic system should be safeguarded. It is for this reason that a debate has been launched in the WTO about core labour standards. On the other hand, the clear evidence that liberalisation has the effect of raising average wage levels must not be forgotten. Nor should the ability of developing countries to retain their right to competitive low wages be threatened by any attempts to harmonise them upwards. If that was the case, concern for labour standards would quickly collapse into a covert attempt to construct new barriers to the participation of developing countries in world markets.

Similarly, there is growing concern that globalisation endangers standards of environmental protection. Again, I would urge those who share these concerns not to regard them as necessitating hostility to globalisation. Both environmental protection and economic liberalisation are desirable objectives, and it is not the case that one must be in opposition to the other. The work already done in the WTO Trade and Environment Committee shows that this is so, even though it has not yet led to effective agreements as to how the two objectives should formally interrelate. Indeed, an open global economy depends upon effective environmental protection if it is to be sustainable. I see a double challenge: to promote intelligent and informed debate on how to pursue both objectives in tandem, and to seek widely accepted multilateral mechanisms which will enable us to maintain the right balance as we do so.

Another common fear is that globalisation undermines national, regional and local cultural values. We live, we are told, in a universe flattened by a Coca Cola and MTV culture in which cultural difference is squeezed into the same homogenised mould and traditional primitive societies are extinguished. This argument requires close examination. I see no inherent reason why the opening of the world economy need subvert diverse cultural values. Naturally, if the economic conditions of life in different parts of the world become more equal, this is likely to be reflected in a greater similarity of lifestyles. In a global economy our cultures increasingly will be exposed to one another. But I see no reason to believe that this should necessarily have destructive or negative consequences. On the contrary, such interchange can be enriching for us all. The greatest culture has often been the progeny of a mix of different values, styles and perspectives. Culture is nothing if it is not fluid, creative and continually reinventing itself in the face of new and diverse influences. It is strangely deterministic, in a way reminiscent of Marxist thinking, to say that economic liberalisation is bound to weaken national cultures because culture is wholly determined by underlying economic forces. Thankfully, social values and culture are more complicated than that and are nourished by more than the soft drinks we consume or the television we watch.

For those who are primarily concerned to safeguard the continued flourishing of distinct European cultures, I would say that whilst it may be legitimate to give public subsidies, for example to the film industry, there is no justification for stopping or limiting the entry of products from other cultures. The best way of preventing subsidies for national culture degenerating into a new form of protectionism is to insist that they should be available to foreign firms, too, provided that they produce products promoting the national culture, for example by making a film in the language of the country concerned, with themes reflecting its culture.

What is abundantly true, however, is that globalisation requires a greater willingness to accept change. Change is not

new, of course. As Heraclitus said 'only change is constant'. But
the forces shaping and shaped by globalisation mean that
change, particularly the ebb and flow of economic cycles, has
come to effect all parts of society. This has the most immediate
effect on the world of work. Full-time employment which can
be guaranteed for life is becoming rare. Increasingly, an individual may jump from one job to another several times during the
course of his or her working life. This may involve spells of
unemployment and shifts between part-time and full-time
work. In some developed countries the situation has become
particularly dramatic, if not extreme. In the United States, for
instance, young Americans aged twenty-five will normally have
held some seven jobs since the age of sixteen, almost one job per
year.

Of course, the increasing fluidity in the labour market can not
be reduced to the effects of globalisation alone. As I have already
indicated, other factors such as technological change and
demography also play a part. But the inter-dependence of
economies means that the competitive pressures for continual
innovation are greater and that the economic upturns and
downturns in one country have a more significant effect than
previously was the case on the economic climate in other
countries.

In order to deal with this whole new environment, a number
of key lessons need to be drawn. What is required is not resis-
tance to a generally beneficial development, but responses which
make the best of it, and which make it understandable and
acceptable.

First, education and training are absolutely essential to the
fortunes and well-being of society. Studies have clearly shown
that education, now more than ever before, is the most important factor determining the employability of the workforce. In
the European Union, for instance, the average unemployment
rate for men of working age who have completed a higher

education course is around 5 per cent. For those who have only a basic level of education, the unemployment rate is at least twice as high. The point is not so much that education, through the knowledge or skills that it imparts, provides access to the job market in the first place, but rather that education provides individuals with the *adaptability* necessary to make the increasingly frequent changes required during the course of their professional career.

But this also means that education should not simply be regarded as a one-off experience for the young at school or university. Rather, in order to learn and relearn the skills necessary to remain active in the changing job market, education and training should be available throughout an adult's life. Above all, this requires a greater alliance between employers and educational bodies to encourage training at the workplace itself and a flexible approach to adult education courses and qualifications.

Second, labour markets must become supple and dynamic enough to accommodate and encourage the necessary fluidity in working patterns. I do not want to rehearse here the detailed arguments about the success of the US and UK economies in creating jobs compared to the sclerotic performance of most continental European economies. Inevitably, particularly as this has become a point of increasing political attention here in the United Kingdom, some of the subtleties have been lost. For instance, there are European countries such as the Netherlands which have made great strides in deregulating their labour markets and have seen a significant growth in employment as a result.

But the underlying point is clear: as long as it is expensive, administratively difficult and fiscally disadvantageous to change jobs, both employers and employees are likely to be cautious about creating new job opportunities. The net result is growing unemployment and a tragic underutilisation of the employment potential of Europe's labour force. Needless to say, the answer is not to remove all social and welfare protection from workers. Rather, it is to make such protection affordable, by stimulating economic growth. To do that it is necessary to enable employers to expand and contract their labour force in keeping with their optimal needs and also to enable employees to carry their own rights to health cover, education, pension and housing when changing from one job to the next. In some parts of the world, where paternalistic employment patterns still prevail, in which housing, education and pension rights are provided by the employer, that is not currently possible. To make it so, a hard look at the way tax benefits are structured is often needed as well as a progressive move towards individual, portable pension and health provision for those active in the labour market. Above all, labour markets must be deregulated, particularly where excessive regulation affects the ability of small and medium sized companies to alter and adapt their employment plans. This is a lesson which the United Kingdom has learned and which other European countries are now starting to follow themselves.

Finally, the pace of change brought about at least in part by globalisation requires that Governments assume a greater responsibility than before to *explain* to their electorates why the continuing pressures to adapt and innovate need to be accepted rather than rejected. Change is, by definition, threatening. But change can only be mastered if we are prepared to adapt and reinvent ourselves too. This is not an easy political message to convey. Electorates turn to their governments for a sense of purpose, predictability and reassurance. The political temptation to retreat into economic, cultural and political certainties is great. In France today a novelist and literary critic with no economic training has managed to sell 170,000 copies of a book entitled *The Economic Horror*[2] which sets out in strident terms why the emphasis on deregulation, change and flexibility should

---

[2] Vivianne Forrester, *The Economic Horror* (Paris, 1996).

be rejected in favour of a return to a protected and stable economic order. The human and political appeal of such thinking is obvious but the argument is desperately misguided since the recommended cure would only exacerbate the symptoms of growing unemployment and insecurity.

In other words, it is incumbent upon governments to explain the forces which require the dynamism and openness of modern economies, however unsettling those forces may appear. This, in itself, requires an unusual degree of modesty from politicians since they need to admit that they are not fully in control of all the factors which influence society's economic well-being. It is often the hubris of politicians, who are tempted to make extravagant and unrealistic claims about their own ability to change things, which leads to the disillusionment amongst the electorate which has become so prevalent.

SOVEREIGNTY

If these are the responses to globalisation that are needed in terms of economic policy and its explanation at a national level, that is not the end of the story. We have already seen that, in the international trading system, the pressure of globalisation has led not only to liberalisation, but also to the creation of a supranational dimension in the dispute settlement mechanism. This is a fundamentally new development reflecting the fact that to accommodate globalisation it is necessary to create a degree of supranational decision-making which in turn, requires a shift in the way we conventionally think about national sovereignty. Sovereignty, of course, means different things to different people. In western Europe, where powerful sovereign nations have jostled with each other for centuries, the issue has become one of to what degree economic and political sovereignty should be pooled for the greater benefit of all. In other parts of the world, however, particularly where nationhood has recently reasserted itself such as in the former Soviet Union, sovereignty is still associated with the straightforward maintenance of a country's territorial and ethnic integrity and bloody conflicts are spawned as competing claims to such integrity are made.

In the United Kingdom, sovereignty has assumed a highly charged resonance. But it is shot through with unresolved contradictions. More than almost any other major country, the United Kingdom is willing to alow foreign companies into the heart of its own economy. During the 1990s, the United Kingdom has received as much inward investment from abroad as Germany, France and Italy combined. This has got to the point where major sectors of the economy, such as the car industry, are foreign owned and even utilities, such as electricity, are being bought up by non-British companies, without arousing any significant opposition. I regard this as a mature response to the emergence of a global economy, with Britain for its part also a major investor overseas. And yet we remain extraordinarily sensitive about even the most modest pooling of political and legislative authority. Why is it that we are happy to reap the benefits of foreign ownership and investment in our electricity, water and rail networks and yet are affronted by even the most innocuous legislative proposals from Brussels?

I do not intend to try to add significantly to the enormous literature already accumulated on sovereignty, but I do wish to stress that sovereignty is not and never has been absolute. As Geoffrey Howe memorably said in his own Rede Lecture in 1994, sovereignty 'is not like virginity, now you have it, now you don't'.[3] Sovereignty is relative. Above all, there is a difference between sovereignty understood as the dry, legal entitlement to make decisions for oneself and a broader concept of sovereignty which focusses on the ability of a country to maximise *effective* influence on the future welfare of its citizens. For instance, if the

3 Geoffrey Howe, *Nationalism and the nation-state*, Rede Lecture, 1994).

United Kingdom were ever to decide to repatriate its authority from the European Union to negotiate international trade agreements with Japan, the United States and others, it would be taking back the strict *competence* to negotiate on its own behalf. But it would lose effective influence over its own destiny. For it would have no more influence in international negotiations than any middle-sized nation-state. By contrast, since it has long since agreed, along with all EU member states, to devolve the authority to negotiate in international trade negotiations to the European Commission, it has the benefit of being part, and an important part, of the largest trading bloc in the world. By surrendering some formal, legal sovereignty, effective real sovereignty has been gained. And as it happens Britain has been able to persuade its partners that the European Union's considerable muscle should be used to advance the liberalising trade agenda that Britain favours.

Interestingly, this perception of the evolution of sovereignty in Europe has begun to inform some of the leading academic studies of the history of European integration. Alan Milward, for instance, astutely entitled his ground-breaking history of the origins of European integration *The European Rescue of the Nation-State*[4]. The idea, though highly complex in historical detail, is relatively simple: in the post-war political settlement in each European country, electorates demanded ever greater economic and welfare returns. European governments found that these returns could most easily be secured by guaranteeing better access to each other's markets and by fully exploiting the advantages of a larger wealth-creating customs union. Of course, there are a number of other important historical conditions which led to the advent of European integration – not least the French political ambition to contain Germany and the

---

4 Alan S. Milward, The European Rescue of the Nation-State (London: Routledge, 1994).

United States' pressure for a unified European bulwark against Soviet power – but the underlying observation is an important one. European nation-states saw that their own sovereignty, the ability to answer to their own domestic needs, could actually, in anything other than a purely legalistic sense, be extended by a fairly high degree of political and economic integration with each other.

But if supranational institutions and decision-making processes are inevitable and necessary in the new globalised economic order, they also have to be politically acceptable, whether such institutions are international or just European. To this end, it is important that institutions such as the World Trade Organisation are seen as means by which transparent and enforceable rules are fairly and evenly applied to the countries participating in the multilateral trade system. The creation of the WTO's binding dispute settlement procedures was a major conceptual leap in this regard. In order that the legitimacy of these new procedures takes root, it is essential that governments, business leaders and opinion formers persuade the public that such rules and procedures are necessary in order to accommodate the process of globalisation smoothly and fairly. Above all, it is important to stress that the new system is based on the voluntary acceptance and respect for common rules and has not been imposed by any one country or group of countries on any other. It is crucial that the fundamental democratic underpinnings of these new supranational arrangements should be well understood. They have been freely agreed to and endorsed by democratically elected governments. It is their responsibility to explain to their own electorates that they are willingly submitting themselves to the new multilateral rules in order to ensure economic fair play in international trade and so maximise the economic benefits for all.

THE EUROPEAN RESPONSE

If, however, the acceptance of a degree of supranational decision-making is a proper response to globalisation on an international scale, where does the 'European response' of the second
half of the title of my talk come in? Could it not be argued that
the evolution of supranational arrangements such as the World
Trade Organisation supersedes the development of European
integration itself?

On a political and institutional level, the answer is straightforward: by coming together and speaking with one voice in the
new supranational institutions, the member states of the EU are
guaranteeing themselves a central role in the evolution of multilateral, globalised economic relations in a way that they would
not be able to sustain on their own. Far from being superseded,
the EU has become a major player in the global arena. The
achievements of the EU in moulding the international trade
agenda stand as some of the most tangible successes of
European integration. The case for pooling sovereignty and
standing strong together rather than weak apart is probably
more obvious in this field than any other. But the pace and
content of globalisation, as we have seen, is changing all the
time, particularly as it has come to embrace services and investment rather than just the trade in goods. It is important that the
European voice is heard as clearly in these new areas as it has
been in conventional areas of international trade. For this
reason, I have been advocating for some time that the legal base
of the EU Treaty should be amended in the on-going Inter-
Governmental Conference to update the ability of the European Commission to negotiate effectively on behalf of the
member states in *all* areas of international trade.

But the challenge of globalisation has implications for
Europe's internal policy, as well as for its approach to the rest of
the world. How should Europe respond to the fact that globali-

sation demands that modern economies should be open to outside investment, have flexible labour markets, be technologically innovative, be able to adapt swiftly to new competitive challenges and possess educational systems which can provide the necessary intellectual and specialised skills for an increasingly mobile workforce? If European integration is based on achieving these aims, then it is answering directly to the needs of the new global economic order. Thankfully, I do believe that is broadly what is happening. The single market, which has created a market of over 370 million of the world's richest and most demanding consumers, has provided an immeasurable dynamic boost to economic activity in Europe by encouraging the spur of competition between companies, accelerated the pace of industrial restructuring, providing a wider range of goods and services to consumes at lower prices and cutting the costs and time of travel. The Commission has recently calculated that the single market has already created between 300000 and 900000 extra jobs and an increase in EU income of 1.1 to 1.5 per cent in the period 1987–93.⁵ It should not be forgotten that the single market is one and a quarter times the size of the US market, and two and a half times the size of the Japanese market.

At the same time, the single market has also remained open to products and investment from countries from all over the world. This has provided the additional motivation to remain competitive with world standards and has led to a significant influx of much needed foreign capital investment into Europe, not least into the United Kingdom.

In other words, the key achievement of European integration, the single market, is not only a highly successful response to the increasing economic interdependence of European countries; it also directly answers to the challenges and opportunities of globalisation.

5 European Commission, *The Impact and Effectiveness of the Single Market*, Oct., 1996).

But there is no cause for complacency. The temptation to retreat into defensive and protective policies in response to the pressures applied by globalisation is as great in the European Union as elsewhere. There are constant calls for Europe to raise discriminatory trade barriers against products from third countries which are perceived to be posing an unfair competitive challenge. There are also a growing number of voices raised in defence of labour market regulation and unrealistically generous welfare provisions on the somewhat spurious grounds that they constitute the core of the so-called 'European social model'. Similarly, special pleading for subsidies and state aid to industries that have not been able to adapt to new market conditions is a repeated refrain heard throughout Europe, as is, of course, the demand for continued unchanging levels of public intervention in support of the agricultural sector by way of the Common Agricultural Policy.

These are not just straws in the wind. They represent a strong strand of opinion which regards economic liberalisation in Europe and globalisation as direct threats to the vested interests and protected sectors of European society. Whilst the fears that underpin such concerns are understandable, if they are allowed free rein they would lead Europe in a direction which would only increase economic insecurity, unemployment and under-achievement. So it is essential that Europe should maintain the current momentum towards liberalisation, dynamism and flexibility.

EUROPE'S FUTURE NEEDS

To that end, I wish to highlight three particular issues which I consider to be essential to Europe's future if we are to have the right degree of integration, and if that degree of integration is to be acceptable to Europe's citizens. First, there has always been a tendency to regard European integration as a process which is constantly on the move and must not be allowed to come to a state of rest. Hence the oft-repeated bicycle analogy: it must keep moving otherwise it will fall. The implication is that with each step towards integration, other steps automatically become inevitable. So the customs union called into being the single market and the single market will call into being a single currency.

I firmly believe there is nothing inevitable about history, and that a bicycle that never stops eventually runs into a brick wall. As Isaiah Berlin has recently so well described, the great system-builders of the nineteenth century – Hegel, Comte, Marx – depicted a world in which societies were subject to deterministic laws.[6] These laws, if properly understood, would provide a predictive explanation of all political and economic development. Strangely, this nineteenth-century thinking is still applied widely to European integration, as if it is obeying immutable and unavoidable laws of human conduct. Thankfully, the world is in reality a messier and less predictable place in which we are freer to determine, for good or ill, our own fates. As Berlin says, the real picture is one 'of men as free, sometimes strong, and largely ignorant which is the precise contrary of the scientific view of them as weak, determined and potentially omniscient'.

There is nothing inevitable about European integration nor is there a fixed road map according to which it should take place. Speaking about European unity in London in 1947, Churchill memorably declared 'Far off, on the skyline, we can see the peaks of the Delectable Mountains. But we cannot tell what lies between us and them. We know where we want to go, but we cannot foresee all the stages of the journey, nor can we plan our marches as in a military operation.'

This is important to stress since it is now sometimes claimed that Europe must begin to explore the possibilities of greater integration in new areas such as tax, social security and labour

[6] Isaiah Berlin, *The Sense of Reality* (London: Chatto & Windus, 1996).

market regulation because this will be 'inevitable' in an increasingly unified single market with a single money. In fact, whilst modest harmonisation might be desirable in indirect taxation, for instance, there is no absolute economic logic which dictates that the single market and the Euro require major further harmonisation in other areas. In other words, it is important that European integration is not viewed as a messianic voyage which must be pursued to its glorious end. This reflects a simplistic reading of history and would lead to a growing tendency towards over-regulation, if not excessive protectionism – exactly the wrong response to globalisation. So the political will which has pushed Europe in the right direction so far must be maintained, and the United Kingdom, with its long tradition of liberal open economic thinking, must remain at the forefront of the debate.

Second, it is urgent for the EU to enlarge itself to embrace the countries of central and eastern Europe. This is a moral imperative because of our responsibility to extend the promise of full participation to those who have been denied their rightful place at the heart of the continent by an aberrant ideological system for a significant part of this century. But it will also ensure that the EU itself is forced to accommodate greater diversity and so benefit from the increased flexibility and dynamism which will follow. Enlargement is by far the greatest challenge facing Europe today, arguably more significant even than the move towards monetary union. Enlargement will shape the Europe of the next century by forcing the pace both of the reform of the EU's own institutional and decision-making processes and of European economic policy. One of the more interesting ironies developing today is that some of the reforms undertaken by governments in eastern Europe, barely freed from the grasp of Communism, are proving to be more progressive and ambitious than the efforts undertaken within western Europe itself. We will benefit at least as much from their membership of the European Union as they will.

Third, subsidiarity. This is a word which has assumed a vague, almost totemic, meaning in the European debate. But the underlying objective, of ensuring that decisions are only taken at a European level where there is added value in doing so, is crucial and must not be forgotten. As globalisation proceeds, as supranational institutions converge and as European integration develops, it is more than ever important that electorates do not feel that they have been cheated of their own power to influence decision-makers. This requires a more subtle division of labour between different centres of power and political institutions. Decisions should be made at their most appropriate level. As Ferdinand Mount has said 'authority must reside and be seen to reside where it is, in theory, supposed to reside. A headmaster should be allowed to act like one. A manager should be left to get on with managing'.7 Similarly, local communities should not feel that local decisions are unnecessarily dictated by national or international strictures. The necessary degree of pooling of sovereignty will only be acceptable if people are confident that their governments will always be vigilant to ensure that there really is something to be gained every time a step in the direction of further integration is taken. Governments entering into international commitments must consider carefully whether the effects of those commitments will not intrude unnecessarily into the minutiae of regional or national practices. The EU must continue to vet any legislative proposal against the real European-wide need being addressed and be sure that the problem cannot be more adequately dealt with at a national level.

Conversely, local, regional and national political institutions should be prepared to accept the need for supranational decision-making bodies when it is patently obvious that they are addressing challenges which can only be effectively dealt with at

7 Robert Devigne, *Recasting Conservatism* (New Haven: Yale University Press, 1994).

that level. In this way, the complex web of authority and institutions which exist below and above the level of the nation-state will become both more comprehensible and legitimate as citizens perceive that those governing them are providing an adequate but not excessive response to the challenges of globalisation.

THE UNITED KINGDOM PERSPECTIVE

Before concluding, I cannot resist making just a few remarks on the implications of all this for the British attitude towards the EU. Needless to say, given my view of the success of the EU so far in pooling sovereignty for the wider benefit of its Member States and in adapting to the challenges of globalisation, it is obvious to me that Britain's own interests can only be served through a continued commitment to the process of European integration. For this to happen, it seems to me necessary to refine the conventional understanding of political sovereignty in the United Kingdom.

Sovereignty in the United Kingdom, in the absence of a written constitution, is wholly invested in the Queen in parliament. Westminster is sovereign and absolute. The power of Westminster as the undisputed centre of authority was fully exploited to push through some overdue and essential economic reforms in the early 1980s and beyond. Indeed, some commentators such as Simon Jenkins have claimed that the exercise of centralised authority in recent times has undermined the unwritten checks and balances on central power.[8] Perhaps this was inevitable or at least justifiable given the degree of change which it was necessary to achieve. None the less, Westminster's sovereignty has certainly long been regarded as out of step with normal understandings elsewhere of the nature of constitutional government.

8 Simon Jenkins, *Accountable to None* (London: Penguin, 1995).

Friedrich von Hayek, for instance, memorably declared that 'Since constitutional government is limited government there can be no room in it for a sovereign body if sovereignty is defined as unlimited power.'9

The question I would therefore ask is whether the traditional view of the absolute sovereignty of parliament is sustainable in the face of the challenges posed by globalisation and the experience of sharing of sovereignty on a European level. Is it really meaningful to talk of the unchecked sovereignty of Westminster when sovereignty has already been to some extent pooled at European and even international levels? Is the formal sovereignty of Westminster not already limited in practice given the dispersal of sovereignty in the real world? Indeed, is there not a danger that if the formal, sovereign competence of parliament is insisted on too much, the reality of a shared and widely distributed sovereignty will be regarded as unacceptable when it is in fact necessary to promote our well-being in today's world? That could only lead to an unrealistic and negative reaction which would be damaging and counter-productive. There is no better place than a university steeped since the days of John Locke in a rationalist, pragmatic, and realistic tradition to plead for a realignment of our constitutional and political rhetoric with the needs and realities of today's world.

CONCLUSION

In conclusion, globalisation is a very real phenomenon which poses substantial challenges to the way we run our affairs both politically and economically. The EU has proved itself as a uniquely effective response to these modern challenges and has enabled nation-states to extend a much greater degree of effective sovereignty over the new international order than they

---

9 Quoted in Devigne, *Recasting Conservatism*.

would have been able to do on their own. At the same time, the understanding of political sovereignty within nation-states such as the United Kingdom must evolve with the new international realities that surround them. Only then can the fears and anxieties of electorates about the rapid pace of change be addressed. If not, the likelihood of the emergence of an increasing number of populist, xenophobic and defensive political movements will be very significantly increased.

The implications of EMU for
Britain and Europe

ooooo

It is not a surefire recipe for popularity in British politics to be a supporter of EMU these days. The Conservative Government has stuck solidly to its approach of wait and see, but it is none the less subjected to a daily barrage of efforts to get it to shift to a less rational, negative stance. I say less rational because, ironically, EMU represents an approach which is wholly in line with Conservative economic philosophy. And there seems to me to be no logic in rejecting ideas which are in tune with Conservative thinking purely on the ground that they come from Europe.

It is my thesis that Economic and Monetary Union is a radical but Conservative idea: it represents minimal government intervention. It promotes free markets. It locks future governments, both here and on the continent, into sound Conservative economics. And it will strengthen Britain in both economic and political terms.

Radical Conservatism has for the last two decades involved shaking up those institutions and relationships which have held Britain back in the post-war period. The Big Bang unleashed the power of the City of London. Privatisation turned sleepy public sector monopolies into world beaters like British Airways, British Telecom and British Steel. NHS reforms have begun to expose hospitals and surgeries across the land to the discipline of the market. On macroeconomic policy too, the Conservative approach has enabled Britain to break successfully with the old habits of boom and bust which were entrenched in the sixties and seventies.

Address to the Ernst & Young dinner in the Banqueting House, Whitehall, 23 January 1997.

Over the past eighteen years, the macroeconomic policies adopted by successive Conservative governments have all been directed towards breaking this vicious circle: from the Medium Term Financial Strategy, dating from the days when Geoffrey Howe was Chancellor and I was Chief Secretary to the Treasury, to shadowing the Deutschmark, joining the ERM, and now inflation targeting. All of these approaches have played their part in Britain's current economic success; although they are not all given equal credit.

The mythology which has grown up around the ERM suggests that it was something of a cuckoo in this nest. Not so; the fact that the ERM was a highly effective external anchor for macroeconomic policy has been overshadowed by our exit from the mechanism. But we should not forget that, in the two years in which we were inside the ERM, interest rates fell by five percentage points and inflation by six percentage points. In the four years since, interest rates have only fallen by a further four and a half percentage points and inflation by less than two and a half percentage points. The gains of abandoning this anchor, which are claimed by opponents of EMU, simply do not stand scrutiny.

Nor can Britain's success at combating unemployment – in comparison with the rest of Europe – be credited to our departure from the ERM. To do so is to underestimate the hugely important structural changes which four successive Conservative administrations have made to the British economy through privatisation, trade union reform, cutting state intervention and creating popular capitalism. These are the policies which have created jobs and made Britain competitive.

Compare the British experience with that of Italy, if further proof is needed. Italy left the ERM at the same time as Britain. It devalued by 40 per cent between spring 1992 and March 1995 and looked to have obtained a significant competitive advantage which would help it grow faster than others still inside the

ERM. But this did not happen. The short-term export advantage gained by devaluation quickly disappeared when it was not matched by real competitive gains. Italy's growth performance since 1992 has, as a result, been worse than that of Germany and France and its unemployment rate has risen from just over 10.5 per cent in 1992 to over 12 per cent in 1996. So let us not sell the achievements of Conservative governments short. Nor should we allow ourselves to be misled into thinking that breaking the European monetary link is the cause of this current success.

Even though we maintained the same broad monetarist approach to policy after leaving the ERM, our departure from the mechanism is instructive. It underlines the fact that all of the sound money policies which we have pursued in the past two decades have been pursued in the face of political pressures trying to weaken them, if not reverse them entirely. These pressures have so far successfully been seen off, but it would be a brave man who would say that this would always happen in future. I simply do not believe that the anti-inflationary culture of recent years is now so deeply embedded in the system that it can be relied on to endure without an external link such as an institutionally integrated Central Bank.

Joining EMU would set a tough Conservative approach to monetary policy in stone and eliminate the risks of reversal. It would do this by giving us a price stability rule. Once EMU gets underway, the body responsible for applying this rule will be the European Central Bank. It will be legally bound to manage monetary policy so that it delivers low inflation. And it will be accountable to the Council of Ministers and European Parliament, but as the bank will be operationally independent, they will not be able to interfere in the day-to-day decisions it makes about interest rates or the money supply.

These are those who complain that these arrangements will be too far removed from the market. They won't be. In many ways they will more closely reflect economic fundamentals than a floating pound. Firstly because speculation will be reduced, as there will be less uncertainty to bet against. And secondly because monetary policy will be tightened and loosened in response to the real behaviour and needs of the European economy.

If this alone were the attraction of EMU, it ought to tempt us, but there is much more on offer. Many of you who do business in Europe know how reliant Britain is on a prosperous European economy. Our livelihoods are now inextricably linked, not just through export performance, but through new investment, mergers, markets for our thriving service industries, and the hundreds of thousands of jobs which EU firms provide in Britain. It is in our interests that Europe continues to thrive.

Consequently, if EMU can help our continental partners then it will help us too. Many European economies need to make urgent supply-side improvements in their economies if they are to achieve their full economic potential. If Europe is to be at the cutting edge of international competitiveness, it needs more flexible labour markets, a smaller public sector to prevent the crowding out of private investment, more competitive utilities. EMU is already helping in all of these areas. In order to get their economies in shape to meet the Maastricht convergence criteria, European governments are, for example, privatising state-owned industries. France has sold off Air France's subsidiaries and intends to seel off France Telecom, Thomson and other state holdings. Measures are being introduced across Europe which will make labour markets less rigid. The Netherlands, Italy, Belgium and Spain have all introduced changes in their employment laws which have made it easier to hire and fire workers and moderate growth in wages. And highly protected markets like telecoms are being opened up to new competition in Germany, France, Belgium and Spain. All of this is desirable in its own right, but it would not happen nearly as quickly, or perhaps at all, if EMU was not in prospect and these measures were not needed to cut public sector deficits.

On top of the benefits of committing ourselves and our partners to virtuous economic policies, there are more direct benefits to be had from EMU. There are the oft-quoted, but often underestimated, reductions with a single currency will mean in the costs of switching into other European currencies. It has been estimated that for the United Kingdom alone this could mean a saving of something of the order of £2–3 billion per year in terms of lower bank charges and company costs of handling many different currencies. This sum is, incidentally, considerably more than Britain contributes to the EU budget each year.

Of even greater significance will be the elimination of exchange rate risk which will bring down interest rates, stimulate business investment and give a further filip to cross-border trade in Europe. This is self evident. Companies in London trade with their counterparts in Manchester far more frequently than they would if there were both a London pound and a Manchester pound. This effect of EMU will be particularly beneficial to small and medium sized industries who want to do business in Europe, but for whom exchange rate hedging is not cost effective.

Last but by no means least, we must take into account the difference which the introduction of the single European currency will make on the world stage. The euro is likely to become a major world currency and could soon find itself sharing in the benefits which the dollar enjoys from being an international reserve currency. This would imply that members of EMU would find that their currency is in greater demand internationally and as a result they would have to borrow less. This will generate further interest rate savings. Moreover, as the euro grows in importance, there will also be considerable international transactions savings on offer. At the moment, about 50 per cent of world trade is invoiced in dollars, despite the fact that the EU has a much bigger share in international trade than the United States. Under these circumstances, it is not difficult to imagine at least some of this dollar dominated trade shifting into euros.

On top of all this, we have to consider the impact of this powerful new currency on global economic policymaking. At present, the United States and the EU have roughly equal shares in industrial country GDP, but the United States has one macroeconomic policy whist the EU has fifteen. When we sit around the table in the G7, OECD or IMF, it is therefore hardly surprising that it is the US voice which makes most impact. This is not in our interests. The United States runs its economic policies to suit itself as it has a perfect right to do. But the sheer importance of the dollar to international trade and finance mean that its policies have a disproportionate, and not always desirable, effect on us. The weakening of the dollar in 1995 for example created a flurry of speculative exchange rate activity in Europe which may have knocked as much as half a percentage point off Europe's growth rate in that year. With the euro we will not only be more insulated from the vagaries of the dollar, we will also find ourselves with a more coherent voice on the international stage and thus more able to advance Europe's interests.

Nothing, of course, is a universal panacea. EMU will not automatically deliver a golden age of economic prosperity. But if we design and implement it wisely, it offers us the best chance we have had so far to break the bad economic habits to which we are addicted, to promote the economics of deregulation in the rest of Europe and give Britain a more powerful international voice.

So if EMU is such an all round good thing, why should Britain wait? Why not sing on the dotted line today? I for one would be delighted if we did. It would, for the first time, give us the opportunity to lock in the gains we have made in recent years and to maintain low inflation and low interest rates. But the British government position is pragmatic, reasonable and understandable – there are still important elements of EMU that remain to be determined. We know, for example, how the single currency will be introduced and what it will look like; but we do not yet know which countries will be members and exactly how monetary policy will be managed by the Central Bank. These decisions will not be taken until spring next year.

However, all the indications are that there will a 'good' EMU. Firstly because the stability pact, agreed in principle by heads of government in December, will ensure that any fiscal convergence must be lasting. Once inside EMU any member country running an 'excessive' public sector deficit of more than 3 per cent will be liable to a hefty fine, unless there is a very good reason for it, such as a serious recession. This must put the lie to all talk of countries fiddling the books so that they can sneak through any convergence criteria line up. With the stability pact in place, it would be in no member state's interest to adopt purely cosmetic changes to its budget, knowing that in future their fiscal chickens will come home to roost. Nor would there have been the full consensus that such rules were needed had member states intended EMU to be a soggy fudge.

Secondly, both the Commission and the European Monetary Institute, the forerunner of the European Central Bank, have done a great deal to prepare the ground well. The Commission has brought forward proposals to ensure the legal continuity of contracts which is essential for a smooth transition. And together with the EMI, it has prepared tough, realistic convergence reports on all the member states – congratulating those who have made progress but equally urging more from those who still have more to do.

The whole convergence exercise is not just a beauty contest organised to see who can meet the criteria for EMU. It is rather designed to ensure that economies are genuinely ready for the competitive challenge of EMU. A country like Ireland, for example, which has done so much to bring its economy up to date and its public sector under control, is now considered by everyone to be well on course to adopt the single currency, even if its debit ratio is over the requisite 60 per cent. This is not because anyone wants to fiddle the criteria. The Treaty does not simply contain figures which applicants have to match; it also requires that those figures should not just be applied like a slide-rule but used to obtain a proper view of what is really happening in the country in question. What is important in the case of the debt/GDP ratio, is that the debt burden should be manageable, so that the country concerned is not overcommitted on interest payments on this debt. A figure alone may be a good indication but it does not give the full picture. That is why the Treaty indicates that consideration should also be given to whether the debt burden is declining and approaching 60 per cent. In the case of Ireland, the Commission, the European Monetary Institute and the Council of Ministers all consider that it should pass the test because its debt ratio has fallen steadily and rapidly from 95 per cent in 1991 to 75 per cent last year.

The EMI's most recent pronouncements on how monetary policy should be run by the Central Bank in stage III of EMU are also instructive. They have taken on board best practice from around the EU – not just from Germany – and, indeed, include the UK approach of inflation targeting in their recommended options. This indicates that Britain has an incredibly important role to play in designing EMU and can influence it if it is prepared to be involved.

Of course, none of this impresses those sceptics who call not only for Britain to rule out EMU but even for the rest of Europe to throw in the towel. But what would happen if Europe decided to abandon the idea? It would condemn us to a period of political uncertainty in Europe unprecedented since the end of the war. For EMU lies at the centre of Europe's economic philosophy. It has played a vital part in encouraging deregulation and liberalisation, albeit more slowly than some of us would have liked. Cast doubt on this consensus and the only result will be economic stagnation or worse. Just as we have begun to reach respectable trend growth rates following the recession, Europe would find itself in economic reverse.

And what price the positive structural reforms that most European economies have begun to enact? Reforms in which Britain has an immeasurable stake because they promise better market access – narrow the gap between Britain and continental Europe on labour market policy and reduce the potential pressure of future European pension liabilities on UK interest rates. It is true that these structural measures are causing squeals of pain from the various interest groups which they affect. We understand this in Britain. We have already experienced it in the early 1980s. By calling for others to abandon Maastricht, we are simply calling on them to abandon policies which have worked for us and are working for other countries following a similar path, such as the Netherlands.

If one believes in the Conservative approach – reducing the size of the public sector, fiscal austerity and structural reform – it is illogical to the point of perversity to demand that our partners abandon the self-same approach, just because it is put in an EU context. Let's not blind ourselves to common sense just because it is associated with Brussels.

Of course, if the rest of Europe goes ahead, Britain still has the choice of whether to go with it. So what would be the consequences of Britain deciding to rule out EMU? It is unlikely that it would mean any real change in actual policy. EMU demands low inflation and good public sector housekeeping. Precisely the agenda which the government has been pursuing in any event. Can there be anybody in Britain today who would choose the alternative, of rising prices and government profligacy?

No, the key practical change would be that by giving up on EMU we would be giving up on a fixed eternal discipline. This would send one message and one message alone to the financial markets. We would be saying quite simply: 'We will try our best to stick to sensible economic policies but we are making no promises.' For the markets, a Britain outside EMU would be a greater inflation risk and would have more volatile exchange rates. The markets would demand a price for this. If Britain stays out of EMU it is inevitable that it will have higher interest rates than its continental partners. Over time, this means lower growth and more uncertainty for business. It also mean higher mortgage costs, a lower standard of living for those on fixed incomes, such as pensioners, and less incentive to invest.

The other clear signal that Britain would send by opting out of EMU is that British interests would carry less weight, as we would not be part of the decision-making core in Europe. Under EMU, the European Central Bank is bound to manage EMU in the interest of the European Economy. If Britain is inside EMU, its interest will count as part of the European whole; outside, they won't. Foreign investors would be discouraged both by this and by the continued risks of devaluation. Legally we would be fully entitled to defend the gains which we have made as a result of the single market and we would have full Commission backing to resist any moves by those inside to discriminate against us. But don't underestimate the probable strengths of those pressures. Also, we would increasingly be squeezed out of a G7 process in which three out of the four European members would be committed to EMU. And the United States and Japan would increasingly look to Europe as a whole rather than individual member states as an interlocutor on economic issues.

There are many, very good reasons why it is in Britain's interests to participate in EMU but, as there are still some uncertainties, it is perfectly logical for the Government not to make up its mind yet on which way Britain should lean. 'Wait and see' has been too easily dismissed as fig-leaf politics. It is much more than this.

Nevertheless, I believe it will become increasingly clear that EMU is likely to be in Britain's long-term economic interests. When we remove our Eurosceptic blinkers we will see that it promotes a Conservative agenda and gives Britain a stronger international voice. We will then surely recognise that it is not in our interests to opt out. But I cannot tell you when that moment will come. The sooner the better for Britain and the better for Europe.

How to make trade liberalisation popular

∞∞∞

INTRODUCTION

In a Symposium made up of so many distinguished experts in economics, my role as the first speaker is to make life difficult for those who will follow. The programme indeed makes this clear: the discussions of the day are sandwiched between presentations by myself and Willy De Clerq, two representatives of hard-bitten political realism in the world of trade policy.

Realism does not mean defeatism. I am a convinced free-trader, and have been doing my bit, both in the Uruguay Round and in countering the recent upsurge of protectionist rhetoric in Europe. Realism means having a strategy in that struggle which will guarantee success. We will succeed in maintaining a powerful constituency for open trade only if we maintain a policy which meets the legitimate concerns of European citizens. Only if we do this can we ensure that the principle of trade liberalisation retains the support of the political middle ground, and that the demagogues do not drain our support in favour of their own theories.

THE PROTECTIONIST TRAP

Those theories are indeed pernicious. The key tenet of the protectionist caricature is that free-trade between countries which are too different one from another would be illogical and unjust, so we should stick to regional trade among similar economies. Then they argue that we should fall back on our local markets because we are weak and naive and incapable of defending ourselves in a dangerous world. Finally, they allege that worldwide market opening would destroy Europe because the

Remarks to the Université Libre de Bruxelles, 8 December 1994.

free flow of investment and cheap manpower in the rising economies would increase our own unemployment.

The first of these theories seems to be the most dangerous and the most ugly. We have tried it in the past. The consequence of bilateralism and of huge tariff increases before the Second World War was to bring levels of trade crashing down and stimulate the growth of extremism in Europe. In 1945 we seemed to have learned our lesson. We set up the GATT and we up the Treaty of Rome to base peace and political cooperation on the firm foundations of economic integration.

I would argue that the 1990s have seen the fruition of those post-war dreams, with the completion of the European single market and last year's successful end to the Uruguay Round. This fully reflects European interests. We are the biggest trading power in the world. We account for one-fifth of world trade in goods. Exports of goods account for a 10 per cent of EC employment, 9 per cent of GDP. Services exports add a third as much again.

Of course, open trade is no bed of roses. The great prize of the Uruguay Round has been won at a time when Europe is only just coming out of recession, and when unemployment is still high. It is perhaps, therefore, no coincidence that we now hear voices raised once more to suggest that competition between ourselves and the 4 billion inhabitants of poorer countries would be dangerous for Europe. I find shocking the xenophobia which underlies this theory. Moral outrage apart, it threatens in hard economic terms to bring us once more to the introversion and decline of the 1930s. For a world trading power such as Europe, this is an unthinkable choice.

LIBERALISATION AT WORK

Nor is retreat necessary. Europe has shown in the Uruguay Round that it can negotiate successfully and as a group, in its own best interests. The first proof of this is the enormous market opening that Europe will gain from the Uruguay Round. All calculations suggest that we are the big winners from the tariff cutting exercise. We are net exporters in all the zero for zero sectors. We will gain from intellectual property protection, better access to public procurement elsewhere and a level playing field for services. But everyone else gains too, of course, both in better access to our markets and in higher growth rates all round.

For this promise to become reality, we need to ensure that these concessions are not only written down but carried into practice. That is the purpose of the so-called illicit practices regulation which I have proposed to the Council as part of the Uruguay Round package. We also need to continue out market-opening efforts: this was agreed at Marrakesh, and will be pursued in the WTO. But the fact that there is more to do should not blind us to our achievements to date.

Nor have those achievements been bought for our competitive exporting sectors at the expense of immediate destruction for everybody else. Agriculture and textiles liberalisation are to be carried forward on a reasonable timescale, with guarantees that the reforms are implemented by our competitors at the same time. That too is good news for Europe and reduces the risk of trade friction.

Finally, and this I think is the most important point for those who fear free trade, the GATT and WTO are not extremist liberal steamrollers. Even the WTO's tighter rules will allow protection against unfair competition. They will also allow emergency safeguard action to give a breathing space for structural adjustment in sectors under severe pressure from surging imports. The WTO has increased the scope for using these instruments, at the same time increasing the obligation of transparency, so that producers and importers everywhere have guarantees against abuse of those instruments.

How to make trade liberalisation popular

This outcome provides cold comfort for protectionists. But they are still hard at work, concentrating an increasing amount of time on peddling their third thesis, that cheap labour elsewhere represents unfair competition for labour in Europe, and that the right for Europeans to invest elsewhere creates an unfair drain on European productive capacity.

The claim of unfairness chimes with the concerns of many European citizens today. It is, I am convinced, a good thing that Europeans are concerned about what goes on not only outside their village or region but in other European countries and indeed worldwide. This level of concern reflects an awareness that economically and politically the countries of the world depend more on each other than ever before. It reflects an awareness that the key issues for our future well-being are also global, notably in relation to the environment. Finally, European concerns reflect the immediate access to current affairs afforded by the mass media, which offer a grandstand view, if sometimes a distorted view, of the most spectacular events around the world.

As the individual looks at the rest of the world, he sees things happening in a different way in distant countries. The instinctive human reaction is to mistrust what is different. Indeed, this reaction is reinforced in a democratic society by the belief that our own social consensus is broadly on the right lines, and should therefore be a model for everyone else.

This mistrust of different policies is likely to be strengthened where our own sovereign right to continue pursuing our own policies is – or seems to be – undermined by open trade. Within the European single market, for example, the liberalisation of barriers to the movements of goods, services, capital and ultimately people has in effect led to competition between unharmonised aspects of economic and political systems.

In this sense, open trade is a check on the unrestricted exercise of sovereignty. That does not make trade a bad thing, but it does suggest that the average citizen needs to be convinced that the assumptions underlying our open trade obligations are acceptable, if we are to rely on public support for a continued open trade policy. In Europe, tight central control of state aids, competition policy and technical barriers to trade is the key guarantee of this level playing field. The guarantees are less strong outside the Union and trade is correspondingly less free.

If free traders are not seen to tackle concerns that the man in the street regards are legitimate, we shall lay ourselves open to protectionist demagogy, as when Europeans alleged that other countries deliberately exploit child labour in order to increase European unemployment. Such arguments are plainly simplistic. The abusive exploitation of the young is abhorrent to Indians and Chinese just as it is to British and Belgians. In Europe, as in Asia, the ILO has had occasions in recent years to pillory departures from universally agreed child labour policies. It is not the case that we disagree on the basic objectives. Nor is it the case that some countries are perfect while others are just not interested. It is, however, the case that there is a problem of child labour and that this problem is a source of concern in Europe and elsewhere. We must tackle that problem and be seen to tackle it in order to convince those who hold ultimate power in a democratic system that open trade is fair trade.

Developing countries often profess to find shocking the application of the notion of fairness to international economic relations. In fact, fairness is an objective implicit in developing country policies just as much as in Europe. Developing country restrictions on foreign investment, for example, reflect a concern by developing country citizens that, unless carefully, controlled, foreign investment will be a tool of foreign exploration.

In Europe, we have at long last come to accept that it is a good thing for foreigners to invest in our countries. When Korea

creates new jobs in England, it is seen rightly as a cause of rejoicing. The same is now true of Japanese investment in France. It
was not always so. And in many developing countries, the
attitudes of twenty years ago in Europe still prevail. Would-be
foreign investors are screened, to ensure that their investment
is in the national interest. The size of their plant, the degree of
foreign control, the intended outlets for the product are all
the subject of careful negotiation. These restrictions are
counter-productive. They reduce the potential for worldwide
investors to make money. They reduce beneficial access to world
capital for the developing countries that impose these restrictions. But despite these disadvantages, it will take another round
of negotiations to secure multilateral liberalisation for direct
investment.

This suggests to me that it would be wrong to sweep aside any
request from a demonstration that open trade policies are fair.
On the contrary, it is perfectly proper to pose the question and
free traders everywhere must have a ready answer. The answer
will not be to impose protection or to use trade as a unilateral
level for adjusting the rest of the world to our own one-sided
views. But in a global economy, there can be no taboos. As the
Treaty of Maastricht makes clear, and as Europe tells all its partners around the world, all issues – from human rights to
economic policy – are legitimate subjects for international
concern and for bilateral as well as multilateral dialogue.

SOCIAL DUMPING AND DELOCALISATION

Let me put this philosophy in the context of the debate on social
dumping, in order to make clear that I argue for a fairness policy
because it is in principle right to do so, not because we expect
material gain to result. Contrary to the protectionists, I do not
believe that action on the social front will bring economic benefits to Europe.

The Commission made absolutely clear that this was its position in last year's White Paper. We said at the time that

> the fear of so-called social dumping would be misplaced if it related to a belief that in certain countries the level of social protection is kept low in order to gain a competitive advantage elsewhere. We should not accept too simple a picture of high wage industrial countries and low wage developing countries. Differences in worker wages alone can be misleading. It is true that modern technology spread much faster and more easily than in the past to different areas of the world. But poor education, low skill levels, low levels of capital investment overall and inadequate infrastructure all offset the possible advantage to be derived from low wages. This is not to say that the Community has no difficulty in competing with labour abundant countries. But European competitiveness is falling not principally because of the impact of international social costs differentials in some sectors, but because we ourselves suffer structural distortion in Europe.

Given the current debate on delocalisation, there is a second passage I should quote, on foreign investment.

> European outward investment has been criticised for over thirty years a a means of 'exporting jobs'. The argument runs that outward investment simply deprives Europe of value added activities, increasing our imports and decreasing our exports. *This is not a correct analysis.* Over 80 per cent of Community overseas investment goes to other members of the OECD. Less than 10 per cent goes to the newly industrialised Asian countries and Latin America. Industrialists who invest outside Europe tend to do

so to supply markets other than their own, reimporting barely 10 per cent of their total intra-company purchases from low salary countries where they have invested.

SAFEGUARDS AGAINST PROTECTIONISM

Yes but, I hear you say, you are playing with fire. It is all very well to reject the threat of social dumping or delocalisation. But if, in the same breath, the Commission accepts that social conditions are a real issue for international economic policy-makers, then the Commission will legitimise the protectionist agenda. This is clear a risk, but one that can be avoided. We have always made clear the Commission's determination that in the social field as in, for example, environmental policy-making, there should be adequate safeguards against protectionist abuse.

What safeguards are needed? A key requirement is that the policy to be pursued should be decided multilaterally, with developing as well as developed countries fully involved. That multilateral policy should include objective criteria against which to assess whether or not individual countries are pursuing a policy in line with their promises. Where there seems to be evidence to the contrary, we should also ensure that there are standards to ensure objective and fair investigation into alleged breaches of international rules.

With these aims in mind, I believe that we should focus on ILO standards as the common criterion for social policy objectives, with ILO and WTO working together to judge compliance.

What should we do with the evidence of compliance? I would say that compliance should be rewarded. It is in this spirit that the Commission's proposal for GSP reform includes a provision for additional trade access for countries respecting international standards on free association, child labour, slavery, bonded labour and prison labour. These constitute a relatively narrow set of core issues on which I think all can agree.

Everyone agrees, at least, what is and what is not acceptable use of prison labour, and we are all, I imagine, against slavery. It may be more difficult to set the precise age threshold by which to define what is and what is not a legitimate use of child labour. If harmonisation worldwide is not possible, then a degree of flexibility will be necessary, but within limits that have been agreed multilaterally and which allow all countries to recognise each others' standards as acceptable, given cultural or even economic variations between them.

Such variations are already recognised in ILO and should help to allay fears that a fairness test would deny developing countries the differential treatment that they have constantly enjoyed in GATT and now WTO. But these variations have to be applied in a dynamic way: we can rightly expect higher standards of social and environmental protection from Singapore than from Somalia. In other words, there can be a measure of graduation in the system.

A final point. The Commission is not suggesting that trade policy instruments bear the brunt of our social or environmental policy objectives worldwide. On the contrary, they can only be one addition to the already extensive armoury of assistance measures used by the Commission in its bilateral and multilateral development assistance programmes. The introduction of social issues into the trade field is not a first-best or self-contained policy for improving social standards worldwide. It is however a potentially useful additional tool, and it is in any case an essential response to concerns on the part of European citizens.

CONCLUSION

I hope that this message is not too discouraging. It certainly should not be surprising. Every economics students knows that

GATT-style trade liberalisation is second best to free trade. But it is a lot better than protectionism. In order to sustain open trade policies and to maintain the liberalising trend of the last fifty years, we have to continue to convince the world's citizens that open trade rules are good for them and fair both to them and to everyone else. Indeed, not just to everyone else, but also to animals, plants and the rest of the world environmental system.

These issues will underlie every aspect of the post-Uruguay Round agenda in WTO. That is why this is a timely symposium, and one whose conclusions I look forward to studying. I hope that your conclusions at the end of today will support my instinct that it is possible and desirable to demonstrate the essential fairness of open trade principles. I believe that this means we can accommodate issues such as labour standards on the WTO agenda. I hope that this symposium will give additional guidance to the Commission as to how to achieve this. First, how do we ensure that developing countries understand our approach and accept it? Second, but perhaps more important, what would constitute a truly secure set of safeguards against protectionist abuse of new rules in these delicate areas? I look forward to your questions, once we have heard Professor Bhagwati.

EU–US relations: a partnership of peoples

ooooo

It is a great pleasure to be here today. This Transatlantic Conference is an original and exciting event. It is also an important step forward for the New Transatlantic Agenda, which we adopted in December 1995 to give renewed vigour and energy to the relationship between the European Union and United States. Our theme is building new links, new bridges, between our peoples. This was one of the four priority objectives we set when we wrote that Agenda, and underpins the whole enterprise.

Why is such a conference necessary? The links between the peoples of the United States and the European Union have always been strong and remain so. Ties of family and kinship have been the very core of our close historical relationship. The tradition of European emigration to the United States goes back beyond the Pilgrim Fathers and has continued ever since. These personal links have endowed our societies with common cultural, religious and philosophical traditions.

Moreover, in this century, the people of the United States twice made enormous sacrifices to fight alongside Europeans in the cause of democracy and freedom. And in recent years we have continued, when necessary, to work and fight together to defend our common values and shared interests. The links between us have been, quite literally, forged in fire.

We shall shortly celebrate together one of the most remarkable examples of American commitment to the security and prosperity of the peoples of Europe. On 5 June it will be exactly fifty years since US Secretary of State George Marshall delivered a brief but memorable speech at Harvard, which led to the establishment of the European Recovery Programme, better

Address to A New Transatlantic Agenda Conference on People to People Links, Washington DC, 5 May 1997.

known as the Marshall Plan. Between 1948 and 1952 the United States made available the equivalent in today's money of over $88 billion to sixteen European countries through a variety of aid and assistance programmes. At the end of this period, total production in the target countries was over 65 per cent higher than at the start. Marshall Aid was not the *only* cause of this remarkable reform and revival. But it was a major contribution. The people of Europe, including some of those present today, or our parents or even grandparents, were the direct beneficiaries.

So of course the historical links between our peoples are strong and deep. We are right to cherish these links. They remain important for our present. But they are not alone sufficient for our future. In his election campaign last year, President Clinton emphasised the need to build bridges to the next century. Some of those new bridges must cross the Atlantic, so that the ties that have bound us together in the past will be renewed for the future. *That* is why we have come together today in the Loy Henderson Auditorium.

There is a particular need to build strong bridges because we are living in a period of rapid change. At the level of international politics, we are still reacting to the upheavals caused by the end of the Cold War, which for all its dangers, clearly bound democratic Europe and the United States together. It has become a truism that international relations today are more unpredictable and confusing. A truism – but also a truth. The United States and the European Union are gradually redefining their roles, priorities and relationships. We are less obviously thrown together by external circumstance.

Change within Europe has been dramatic. The artificial division between democratic and communist states has been swept away, and Europe is in the process of being healed. At the time of the Marshall Plan, the peoples of half of Europe were denied access to American economic aid. It is now both a moral duty and a joy for us to assist them to share in the prosperity and democratic stability which the Marshall Plan helped to entrench. As a result of this process, the European Union stands on the threshold of a further enlargement of great historical significance.

The United States is also changing. The economic and demographic centre of gravity has shifted to the south and west – away from Europe. I recently read an estimate that, in twenty years time, one in every three Americans will be of non-European descent. I join President Clinton in rejoicing in America's diversity. This has always been one of the greatest strengths of the United States. In the future, it is common values and aspirations, rather than common ancestry, that will unite us across the Atlantic.

Changes which are happening remarkably fast within both our societies also affect the way we relate to each other. International relations are no longer the exclusive preserve of politicians, diplomats and soldiers. A political elite can no longer dictate how individuals view other countries. Each of us can now have direct access to information from all over the world, through telephones, faxes, affordable international travel, e-mail, and the Internet, and so our societies interact in complex and various ways. These days, to borrow a phrase, we all 'just do it'.

For all these reasons this conference is necessary. I welcome the fact that its agenda has not been dreamt up by a group of men in grey suits, but has evolved directly from contacts between different groups of men and women from all walks of life. I expect that we will leave tomorrow with a practical agenda of genuinely useful follow-up action.

ECONOMIC LINKS

Let me now take a broader look at our economic and political relations. Until quite recently, on both sides of the Atlantic,

Cassandras were crying out that Europe and the United States were condemned to drift apart. I have never accepted this, although it is as well to be alert to the risk. We should guard against the simplistic argument that the removal of a common external military threat removes the whole basis of our relationship. The New Transatlantic Agenda, which covers a broad range of our political and economic interests, is already showing conclusively the benefits of a forward looking, practical and constructive approach.

The United States and the European Union are by far each other's major economic partner. In 1995 they accounted for some 19 per cent of each other's total trade in goods. In services the figures are even more striking: more than 31 per cent of US trade in services in 1994 was with the EU. The figure in the other direction was almost 39 per cent. The trade relationship is not only only large, but it is also largely balanced. For American companies, the European market is four times bigger than Japan. Secretary Daley recently observed that one in every twelve manufacturing jobs in the United States is in a European-owned factory. We also have by far the largest investment relationship in the world. The EU accounts for nearly 66 per cent of all foreign direct investment in the United States, and receives some 45 per cent of total US foreign direct investment abroad. Quite simply, we are involved with each other in a way which eliminates disengagement as a rational policy option.

Those in the United States and in Europe who advocate policies of economic introversion and isolationism as a response to the new challenges of globalisation are profoundly wrong. Together, the United States and the EU account for over one third of world trade in goods, and almost half of world trade in services. Without that trade, world prosperity, and our own, would collapse. I readily accept that the affluent societies of the United States and the European Union face uncomfortable challenges from globalisation. But introspection and the pursuit of economic autarky are not viable long-term options. Meeting and responding imaginatively to the challenges of an open, global economy is the way to advance our interests. We both stand to benefit from a multilateral economic system, in which the voluntary acceptance of common rules permits steady progress in opening markets. The World Trade Organisation is the cornerstone of such a system.

In our bilateral economic relationship, the highest medium-priority is to make a reality of the new transatlantic marketplace. Its purpose is to identify and remove more barriers to trade between the United States and the European Union. In doing so we should be able to generate new trade worth many billions of dollars. In doing so we will also be exploring a new frontier in transatlantic trade relations, going beyond the lowering or removal of tariff barriers to tackle the impediments caused by different regulatory controls and domestic standards. This is not an easy challenge. It requires us to build confidence in each other's regulatory procedures. The first important step will be the completion of an Agreement on Mutual Recognition of standards in a number of sectors, which has now been under negotiation for some time. We must make every effort to achieve this at the EU–US Summit in The Hague later this month.

It is particularly appropriate, at this conference, to draw attention to the Transatlantic Business Dialogue between leaders of major contributions in the EU and the United States. This has proved to be an important catalyst for progress in our economic relations. It allows our business leaders to develop common priorities and to pursue them effectively with governments. It is a very pertinent example of how non-governmental actors can influence the EU–US relationship. I am strongly attached to the continuation of the TABD and hope it will carry on producing important recommendations, such as those that led to our work on information technology and the Mutual Recognition Agreement.

No relationship can be one of perfect harmony, and I cannot avoid striking one discordant note. It is the EU's commitment to an open, multilateral economic system which underlies our opposition to recent legislation introduced by the United States with extraterritorial effects damaging to our legitimate economic interests. After intensive negotiation, we have been able to reach an understanding which has averted a crisis over policy towards Cuba, Iran and Libya. This understanding, in which each side has made undertakings to work on disciplines and principles concerning new investment in illegally expropriated property and the problems caused by conflicting jurisdictions, it is not in itself a final answer to the problem. The European Union is ready to work for a comprehensive settlement, but we will not abandon our opposition to unilateral secondary embargoes.

POLITICAL LINKS

While our links in the private sector are of growing importance, governments still have the ultimate responsibility to develop and manage our relations in ways which ensure a peaceful, secure and prosperous environment for our peoples, and make us effective partners in wider international affairs. I am confident that political leaders on both sides of the Atlantic remain committed to the relationship, as the New Transatlantic Agenda proves. The United States also continues to invest important resources an energy in promoting democracy, economic development and security in Russia, the other countries of the former Soviet Union and the countries of central and eastern Europe. The US contribution to bringing peace to the former Yugoslavia and promoting stability in the Balkan region is also especially important.

This involvement reflects a welcome recognition that the United States' security continues to be bound to the security of

Europe. This is a lesson of history well learned. It is therefore both natural and right that the United States should wish to play a leading role in questions affecting European security, including the reorganisation and enlargement of the NATO alliance. We recognise that the United States remains the most powerful member in that alliance, although the voices of the other members must also carry due weight.

For their part, the leaders and people of the United States should recognise that the Europe we are still rebuilding, in the spirit of the Marshall Plan, is growing continually stronger and more cohesive. The United States helped Europe stand on its feet after the devastation of World War II. You encouraged us to unite. We are increasingly doing so, essentially through the European Union, with its single market, common policies and common institutions. The EU was not so long ago a vulnerable infant. It has now become lusty adult. That is my essential message to you today. With vision and foresight the United States helped put us on our feet. It is inevitable that we should now face the United States as an increasingly equal partner, sharing world leadership more and more as we develop still further our own capacity to act together in a united and effective way. That will not always be comfortable for the United States. But the vision of the Marshall Plan foresaw, clearly and rightly, that the common interests of Europe and the United States were so great that they tipped the balance overwhelmingly in favour of nurturing a strong Europe.

We are already seeing that, in some respects, it is even true that the European Union has assumed the main leadership role, especially in our continent. It is natural that should be so and it should not be a cause of concern, as we exercise that role in directions which reflect our common interests. It is the European union that has led the effort to rebuild the economies of central and eastern Europe. Between 1990 and 1996 the EU and its member states provided more than $58 billion in assistance to central European countries, compared with $12 billion given by the United States. The EU also mobilised more than $80 billion in support of political and economic reform in eastern Europe and the New Independent States of the former Soviet Union.

This European aid can be regarded as a modern equivalent of the Marshall Plan, and was inspired by it. Firmly supported by the United States, it is helping countries build the sort of societies and economies they will need to become eligible for EU membership. The formal process of further enlarging the EU will begin next year, when accession negotiations will start with a number of applicant countries. We cannot predict exactly how fast this enlargement will proceed. Its pace will be determined by the existing members' judgement of the readiness of applicants to meet objective requirements. That is a decision that only we can make, however legitimate the interest of others in the process may be. It is not something that can be rushed ahead out of purely political considerations: joining the EU involves a high degree of economic integration. The stakes are high both for the applicants and for the existing members.

The EU will also grow stronger in other ways. The introduction of a single currency among a large group of EU members will equip the world's largest trading area with a powerful international currency to match its economic weight. Indeed, the euro area will have commercial and economic weight comparable to that of the United States. Even if international use of the euro were simply proportional to present use of the deutschmark, some 30 per cent of world exports would be invoiced in euros. More trade, debt and investment is bound to be denominated in the euro. It will develop into a major world currency, and a strong competitor to the dollar and the yen as a global reserve currency. Europe will therefore become a still more powerful global player and partner.

Even before this, in the area of trade, Europe has been a fully equal partner with the United States in advancing the opening up of the world economy. That was true in the GATT Uruguay Round. It has been true in the achievement of the Information Technology Agreement, removing barriers to trade worth over $500 billion. It has been true in the recently agreed deal to liberalise telecommunications services internationally. Two years ago, for the first time, the European Union stepped into the breach to save a new limited deal to open up international financial services, at a time when the United States was not ready itself for full participation in this endeavour. We hope that this year the United States will be able to work with the rest of the world to achieve a comprehensive, permanent deal in which the United States, as well as Europe, can be an active participant.

The institutional structure of the European Union and its common policies will also continue to develop. The intergovernmental conference, which is due to end in Amsterdam next month, will take important steps to improve the way the Union conducts its business. But I emphasise that this will not be the high water mark of the European Union's ambition to build strong common foreign, security and defence policies. We still have further to go and are determined to get there, in spite of the complexities and difficulties facing us. It is in the interests of both Europe and the United States that Europeans should be able to act rapidly, independently and effectively when the circumstances call for such action. It is also in our interests that we cooperate constructively when we have differences in approach, for example on the best way to deal with Iran – an issue on which the European Union took strong and pointed action last week.

To sum up, ladies and gentlemen, we believe that the New Transatlantic Agenda will allow us to create a partnership of equals, firmly rooted in the common interests and values of the peoples of the European Union and the United States. The personal links we establish in a conference of this sort are bricks to build such a relationship. There is more to do to achieve our goal. But together we have made a promising start. We must go further, because it is through a strong, confident partnership of equals that Europe and the United States will be able to continue to give global leadership.

Towards a Europe for the individual

ooooo

INTRODUCTION

Jean Monnet once wrote: 'Nous ne coalisons pas les Etats, nous unissons les hommes.' We are not allying states, we are bringing together people. Although his original vision was one of states working with each other, and of common institutions which would supervise what the countries agreed to put into the common pot, he came increasingly, as he watched the European Community grow, to believe that he had made a mistake. He came to believe that he should have started with individuals – that the right way into European integration lay through people. 'If I were to begin again,' he wrote on a later occasion 'it would be with education'.

I wonder how he would have seen today's EU from that perspective. What would he have made of the debates about national sovereignty, about the possibility of having a common currency without having a federal state? In some ways he would no doubt have regarded them simply as misplaced – the death throes of the dinosaur nation-state. But in other ways, he would no doubt have understood the profound attachment which people have to their own nation – to which their allegiances and jealousies are so firmly attached.

So tonight I would like to look at what the EU does for the individual. The benefits which the individual gets from Britain's membership of the EU are, I believe, manifold – but they are largely unsung. The strident choirs of eurosceptics and euro-philes chant their sometimes harsh counterpoint in ways which sometimes seem as detached from the real world as the ethereal

The Girton College Founders' Memorial Lecture, Girton College, Cambridge, 17 February 1995.

voices of boy choristers in the Christmas services from King's. So tonight, I propose to try a *bel canto* of my own.

JOBS

The first benefit that any individual looks for in today's world is a job. Leaving aside personal qualifications for the moment, jobs are dependent first and foremost on the general level of economic growth, but a range of specific elements come into the equation as well – the competitivity of businesses in their own markets, the strength of the wider market and the extent to which the 'playing field' is fair and level. The EU makes a clearly positive contribution to the welfare of the individual in each of these areas.

As regards economic growth, Britain is very dependent on trade for its growth and on the EU market for trade. Some 60 per cent of our export goods go to the EU countries – and one in ten jobs depend on exports. We need unimpeded access to the German or the French markets. Businesses need to be able to count on access to those markets when they invest, when they design their products, when they decide on strategy for the future. Jobs depend on those markets. Obviously, other EU countries also want access to them – as they do to our market. And that is healthy in two ways – first, because it widens consumer choice and brings down prices (and examples of this are legion); but secondly, because it also means that our own goods have to be competitive not only in the domestic British market, but also in the European Union and thus in the wider world. The pressure to be competitive caused by the openness and size of the European market is a major contributor to the strength of the British economy and its ability to provide jobs.

So long as competition is fair, British businesses can only gain, and British jobs be secured. But some competition is not fair – and businesses have to be protected against unfair competition, or the jobs and the other benefits they bring to society will be lost. The EU is a stronger protection against unfair competition than Britain alone could ever be, whether that competition is internal to the EU or external in the wider world.

Inside the EU, although the internal market is nearing completion, it needs constant vigilance to see that it really works. All member countries of the EU subscribe to the theory that they should not discriminate between the products and citizens of member all states; but all of them have a sneaking temptation to tilt the balance ever so slightly in ways that will help their own people, and make life just that little bit more difficult for imported products, even when these do come from inside the EU. There is only one body that can act as a policeman, and that is the European Commission. It constantly pursues member countries who do not fulfil their obligations in regard to fair trading conditions, who seek to tilt the balance of trade in favour of their own industries. That task is of crucial importance to Britain. If we are denied fair play, British jobs will be lost. That is only one of many reasons why, if the Commission did not exist, it would have to be invented. A few examples will show how creative countries can be in taking measures which – fair and even-handed though they may appear – are actually designed to be discriminatory and to keep the foreigners out!

A few years ago, the Greek government imposed a ban on the advertising of toys on television unless they were of Greek manufacture – and thus, it said to the Commission, could be relied upon by security-conscious Greek parents and toy-buyers as perfectly safe. The real reason, so the European toy-manufacturers said to the Commission in their complaint, was that there had thus far been very little import penetration in the Greek toy market, and the Greek government was determined to keep it that way. Aha, said the Commission to the Greek government, after investigating the toy-makers' complaint – but if EU toys have the 'CE' mark on them, then they will be safe anyway – so lift the ban! After a little hesitation, the Greeks caved in, and toy exports from this country to Greece became first a possibility, and then a fact.

A different example can be seen in an affair which involved a British shipping company which wanted to run a service between Spain and Morocco. The difficulties placed in their way by the Spanish authorities were tremendous. First, they said that the port from which the service was to be run did not have the capacity to allow an extra line – though it patently had enough capacity to allow the local Spanish shipping company to increase its own sailings. So the British company offered another Spanish port. This one, said the Spaniards, did not have the required customs and immigration service – but then, asked the British company, how are other companies able to run international services to and from it? Ah well, said the Spaniards, they are all coming from inside the European Union – not from outside it. Your port is not designated as a port of entry from third countries under the Schengen Convention, which governs frontier movements. True, said the British company – but all it takes to change that is a letter from you. And so it went on. Eventually, the Commission had to lean on the Spanish government, and the matter was finally agreed – but only because the Spanish government knew that once it came to Court, they would lose.

In another case, the Italians had a special tax on imported cars with more than two cylinders – just one part, it must be said, of a very complex web of arrangements to discourage the import by private citizens of cars bought elsewhere in the European Union. But the way this particular tax worked put special burdens on the manufacturers of imported luxury cars, with clearly discriminatory effects. Put bluntly, it meant that the sales of Jaguar cars were significantly more difficult than they should have been. The result of Commission intervention is that the tax is in the process of being removed.

As to exports outside the European Union, the case is, if anything, even clearer. The role of the European Union, and in particular the European Commission, in advancing trade to the benefit of European jobs is paramount. When I negotiated the Uruguay round on Europe's behalf in 1993, I could not help but notice how much stronger we were as twelve than Britain – or indeed any Member country – would have been alone. The strength of being part of the world's largest trading block enabled me to ensure protection of Britain's interests, just as I could for the interests of other member countries. And at the same time, I could ensure that the general principles we thought were right were there in the final text.

Two examples, both affecting Britain, show how this worked. First, we had a major negotiation on financial services – where Britain is a world leader. Indeed, we still have these negotiations, since the final deadline has been extended to the end of June this year. But although the precise commitments made by each country have yet to be finalised, the principles have already been agreed. Here, we have achieved a major non-discriminatory market opening exercise – and the phrase non-discriminatory is crucial here. We have stopped the Americans from trying to negotiate a series of bi-lateral agreements which would have served US industry fine, but would have completely excluded EU companies from their benefits. We have instead won a substantial wealth-creating exercise world-wide, with substantial incidental benefit on jobs here in Britain. And not just the jobs of Directors of City Merchant Banks, let me add! The Financial services sector is much broader than that, and geographically much wider-spread as well.

At the other end of the industrial spectrum, we have won time for the textiles industry to restructure itself and to find new markets for a restructured industry to win. In Victorian times, the British textile industry supplied the world. I do not think that we shall ever get back to those days, but in the fields where the British textile industry has something to offer, it now has ten years' guaranteed protection to complete its restructuring efforts, but also an enlarging world market opening up for speciality and fashion textiles – that is, the sectors with better qualified jobs and higher added value. World tariffs in the textile area have traditionally been very high, particularly in the developing world, even though the potential for imports there is largely in more expensive or technically more advanced fabrics than they themselves produce. The Uruguay Round has started a process of tariff reduction – sometimes quite substantial – that can only help our industry look forward with confidence.

We have also introduced legislation to enable businesses who think they are being unfairly discriminated against by third countries or find the playing field tilted against them by governments giving unfair subsidies to their own businesses, to get redress. The World Trade Organisation, to which all major trading nations including the EU, the United States and Japan have signed up, has new and strong procedures to settle disputes between parties, and in the EU we have put in place a legal system under which businesses can come to the Commission and make the case for these to be used on their behalf. These new rights mirror the existing rights that businesses have to complain to the Commission if imports are being dumped on the UK market – that is, if goods are being sold here at less than they are sold in their home market, and injury to British business is the result. We have speeded up the time taken for such complaints to be processed, and we shall not be backward in pursuing cases which seem to us to be well founded. These improvements in our trade regime are not the stuff of headlines, but they improve economic prospects and therefore job opportunities in every member state of the EU, and of course particularly in the United Kingdom.

None of these benefits would have been available if we had not been part of the EU. I cannot convert that by a simple arithmetical formula into 3,000 jobs saved here and 4,000 created there. I cannot identify the individual jobs. But they are there. No one can argue against the fact that jobs in Britain have been saved and created by the strength that our membership of the EU brought us in the Uruguay Round.

Another area where membership of the EU has contributed to jobs is in the substantial investment that has flowed into Britain. Britain is the top destination for external capital coming into Europe – because we have a well-educated workforce, because our legislative framework is sufficiently flexible to encourage investors – but above all, because Britain is in the EU and products from factories here can be sold anywhere in the EU, the EEA and wider still. Some cases make a big splash in the news – when Samsung decided to invest £600 million in new factories in Cleveland, for example, everyone could read about it in the press. Most inward investment, even where the sums are quite substantial, goes unnoticed. Just looking a few miles around the Wynyards Development where Samsung are basing themselves, there are hosts of other smaller examples to be found. Let me give you a few. Within the last two years, Goldstar has invested £25 million in Sunderland. Lucas/SEI (a UK–Japanese joint venture) invested £3.5 million, again in Sunderland. Europe Magnetics invested £25 million in a floppy disk plant at Cramlington. Black and Decker invested £7 million in a power tool plant. TRW Transportation Electronics invested £8 million at Houghton-le-Spring. These are all within a very short distance of the Samsung investment. How much more is there across Britain as a whole?

And what about the future? Samsung have agreed to buy a substantial number of memory chip wafers from NEC in Scotland. They are looking round Europe for a site to build a new semiconductor plant, at an estimated cost of $1 billion. Britain must be towards the top of their list for sites for this new $1 billion investment. Would we have even a chance if we were not in the EU? And would our chances be substantially diminished if it were thought likely that Britain would be left behind in Europe, because it relegated itself to a position as a semi-detached member of the EU?

Of course, there are some who argue that all this inward investment is harmful. The jobs created are unreal, they argue, and will make others melt away like fairy gold in the harsh light of day – or at least, so I read in a recent edition of *The European Journal*, the perhaps unlikely-sounding editor of which is Mr William Cash MP. I think few people would agree with him. Most people will recognise that the arrival of high-technology jobs, particularly in an area where jobs of any sort are more than scarce, can only be a good thing. As for the idea that these jobs will simply displace others, I would be more inclined to think it plausible if there were other, less productive jobs in the same or competing sectors. Mr Cash's journal does not list them, and I do not know of any. And even if there were such jobs, would they in turn have been provided in a Britain outside the EU?

Those two examples both concern companies, and companies are the major providers of jobs. The European Union can work for individuals as well, however. For example, a British cellist complained that Greek law barred her from being employed as a cellist by the National Opera of Athens. The Commission looked into her case, and found that Greek law was clearly discriminatory. It is now being changed. Similarly, at Verona University, an outraged British lecturer found that he could be taken on only as a temporary lecturer – permanent posts were reserved for Italians. here, too, the Commission intervened and that discriminatory arrangement has been changed.

I am certainly not claiming that everything in the internal market is perfect. But I have mentioned a few examples to show how an impartial policeman is needed to ensure that it can work evenly for all of us! But in one area, in particular, the EU has shown that it can impose a level playing field even in the most difficult cases, and that is in its control of state aids. This unlikely title hides the habit which certain governments have – or, increasingly, had – of dishing out subsidies to their own industries to keep them in business when their own management had failed. This sounds fine – you stop bankruptcies, you retain jobs: but all at the expense of the taxpayer and at the expense of jobs elsewhere in the EU. Any well-run business expects to compete with other businesses. But none expect to compete with the financial resources and tax-raising powers of a national government determined to keep its lame ducks waddling on.

National subsidies such as these are now generally regarded as out moded – all member countries of the EU have now recognised that, in the long run, they do more harm than good. However seductive they may appear at the start, once going down that road it takes a good deal of self control to avoid ending up in the position in which the Italian government found itself a few years ago, where its industry was dominated by state-owned or state-supported companies in the real world, and its national budget was weighed down with the debt-interest and the subsidy costs of supporting them.

Nowadays, however, as a result of the strictness of the EU rules, subsidy levels in member countries have been falling for a number of years now. The absolute level is still high in Italy but it is coming down; and it is worth noting that it has fallen by half in France, and that across the EU as a whole, levels are substantially lower in real terms than they have been for many years. That goes unnoticed in the press; but it does mean that life is easier for companies in those countries – like Britain – which do not have a tradition of handing out large sums in state largesse.

The prominent cases coming to the Commission these days are undoubtedly those of the airlines. Britain privatised British Airways some years ago – and BA has prospered since. It has shaken off the sluggish habits induced by state ownership, it has used its freedom to borrow on the markets, to increase its capital as need be – and has as a result of that and of real staff and management commitment, increased its productivity to such an extent that it is one of the world's most profitable and competitive airlines. Alas, that cannot be said of many of the flag carriers of Europe. Indeed, even that expression flag carrier has overtones of national pride and sovereignty, to be protected at all costs.

And the cost has indeed been high for some airlines. During the early 1980s, when the travel market was booming and the revenue was pouring in, they did well. They acquired companies elsewhere, and they acquired all sorts of other things as well, starting very often with other, equally unsound, airlines and going on to hotel chains, entertainment firms, and so on. When the cold winds of recession began to blow through the airline business, they turned to their national governments begging for yet another injection of their drug, another capital restructuring or national subsidy.

The Commission had to decide whether to allow this to happen or not. It did not want to decimate the airline industry in Europe – but nor did it want to deal unjustly with regard to those companies which have been through the pain with their own efforts and come out on top. It therefore came up with a policy known as one time, last time. It would allow national subsidies for airlines one last time - only – on the condition that they carry out at the same time proper restructuring programmes which would bring them back into profit, and that they contribute to hauling up their own socks by shaking up their productivity and selling off any assets which are peripheral to the airline business. But you will have seen from the press that the Spanish airline Iberia has just come back to the Commission asking approval for its second last time subsidy from the Spanish government. The case is still being examined at technical level at present, and will come to the Commission only in a few months' time, but it is clear that the Commission's credibility is at stake. It is essential that we should show ourselves ready in this area as in others to take the robust but difficult decisions needed if we are to continue to be seen as the guarantor of fair competitive conditions to European Industry.

To be effective in this respect the Commission also has to deal with unfair monopolistic practices, as well as straight subsidies. These are particularly prevalent in air transport. Monopolies on particularly profitable routes, for example, monopolies on the servicing of aircraft at international airports, or in the handling of freight, or of passenger baggage. Great creativity has been shown in identifying profitable sectors where foreigners should be kept out. We have to exercise similar creativity and vigilance in protecting the interests of European citizens and air travellers.

Tobacco monopolies have also been wide-spread – and not for the health reasons which some governments have latterly invoked. Only now, for example, is the French government privatising its national tobacco monopoly, which controls not only cigarette making in France but also matches. It should be the smokers' dream share!

Nor, indeed, is the EU's contribution to jobs limited to these trade and business measures. The EU also intervenes more directly on the labour market, in particular through the European Regional Development Fund, and through the European Social Fund. The Regional Fund does not make grants to private firms – it helps public projects such as industrial zones, motorways, power and telecommunications infrastructures. Hundreds of millions of pounds have been paid through the Regional fund on such projects in Britain, all with one aim: they are designed to upgrade the efficiency of industry and production in this country. Similarly with the European Social Fund – the EU's training and skill up-grading fund. Here, the EU has been supporting retraining activities for those in need of jobs, whether long-term unemployed or those who have only recently come onto the labour market. It has also begun to fund anticipatory projects – those where one can foresee that a particular group of skills which are still useable now, will become outdated soon. Anticipation means that the workers involved can have their skills improved and reoriented in advance, rather than go through the harrowing experience of being made redundant and having to start afresh from there.

I have gone in some detail into how important it is to keep the internal market of the EU level, and how much benefit we get from our strength as part of the EU when negotiating trade matters, because this is where the fundamental benefit to the individual of Britain's EU membership lies. Given our geographical location, Britain is inevitably going to be part of the European market , and is going to be stronger for that. It is fashionable to decry the European market as old and feeble, and to compare it disparagingly with the vigourous thrusting economics of the Pacific Rim. I do not accept that criticism at all. Those countries have growth prospects available because they start from so far behind us – and because the expectations of their societies – in terms of health care, of pensions, of social security – are also way behind ours. This rapid growth phase will bring them up to levels nearer our own, and thus make them better markets for our own higher technology and higher added-value goods. The level of growth that the EU can achieve is certainly less than theirs, but it will be sufficient to enable us to increase the total throughout society. Outside the EU our domestic economy would inevitably be less stable, our currency more subject to the attacks of speculators, and our interest rates higher. Indeed, if our partners do create a single currency and we decide, when the time comes, to stay out, it is likely that we would pay an interest rate surcharge as a result. Investors will want higher interest rates on the pound than they will on the single currency, to cover the risk of depreciation against the dominant single currency.

A stable economy on the other hand, equals more stability on the job market. Better jobs, and more permanent ones, are the result of our being inside the EU. Whether it is a matter of markets for our own products, of inward investment from outside companies, the greatest benefit that the individual citizen of this country gets from the EU is that there are more jobs available than there would be if we were outside.

QUALITY OF LIFE

But the benefits that the individual receives from Britain's EU membership are not just related to jobs. The EU is also a major contributor to the quality of life that people in this country enjoy, even though they may not notice it.

One simple example of where the EU plays a significant role which most people do not see is in the field of Equal Opportunity between Men and Women. Most people would say: we have our own law – we have the Equal Opportunities Commission, we have a very efficient system of our own and do not need the EU pushing its nose in. But it is not as simple as that.

If you discuss these things with a member of the Equal Opportunities Commission – something I have the pleasure of doing regularly, since my wife is one – you will soon find that Article 119 of the Treaty of Rome is fundamental to the Equal Opportunities Commission strategy. Article 119 is short. It sets out that each member state should ensure the application of the principle that men and women should receive equal pay for equal work. It then goes on to define pay as including all sorts of benefits received from the employer, whether in cash or in kind; whether directly or indirectly.

That article has meant that women up and down Britain have been able to get equal pay for equal work, even beyond what our own legislation provides for – where, for example, the work is not identical, but is rather of equal value or equal type. It has also – and this is potentially a more revolutionary step yet – led the European Court of Justice to rule that equality of opportunity must be applied to pensions as well as to pay – since pensions are in effect deferred pay. The Barber judgement, and the judgements on related cases which followed it, set out broadly that it is illegal to differentiate between pension ages or benefits for men and women. That represented a considerable change for British law (and indeed for the law of most of the member countries). It advances the position of women substantially, over and beyond what British law would have provided, and it did so simply by applying the Treaty of Rome to an individual case brought by a British individual.

Another area where individuals benefit from EU involvement is that of the environment. The environment – particularly when new roads and motorways are to be built – is one of the few causes left able to generate substantial civil commotion in this country. It is one of the few things people care about that much. So they do in other countries. That is why Britain together with its partners have agreed on a substantial body of Europe-wide legislation to protect the environment. But that legislation recognised that it is not for the Community as such to determine particular cases. Matters of land use and town planning are obviously best decided locally. What was felt to be reasonable, however, was to provide that for certain specified types of development, an environmental impact assessment should be carried out, and should be made available to members of the public.

The result of this has been a considerable improvement in the openness of official and governmental bodies when dealing with planning applications, and a greater obligation upon would-be developers (particularly of large industrial or similar sites) to have their plans looked at from the environmental point of view. The directive sets out a range of areas that must be covered in the impact assessment: impact on flora and fauna, on landscape, geographic and geological aspects, and so on. Its beneficiaries are chiefly the citizens of the EU – it provided in all cases for an increase in the information they could rely upon getting where major developments were planned.

Similar increases in information available to the consumer have come about in other areas – for example, in labelling of foods, or in the additives and colourings which can be used as part of manufactured foods. Shops today have a far wider choice of goods available than they had twenty years ago; and the ingredients that go into them have been checked to international standards. Those standards are of course so designed that the goods are safe. But they also encourage trade, as their observance enables goods produced in one part of the EU to circulate freely throughout the Union.

Another way in which the EU has contributed to increasing the quality of life by keeping prices down. That is not, I know, something which is immediately associated with the EU in the public mind – but it is none the less a definite result of the way in which it has run its anti-trust policy over the last decades.

Every member country has some form of anti-trust authority – some of them are serious and professional bodies,such as the UK's own Office of Fair Trading and Monopolies and Mergers Commission. Others, it has to be said, are somewhat more rudimentary. All member countries agree, though, that there are certain issues for which a national jurisdiction is not enough – and where a degree of European supervision is therefore required. Trans-frontier mergers, or mergers of multi national companies with activities in more than one country, are a case in point. When ICI and Dupont, both of which are major multinational companies whose activities go far beyond the borders of the EU, let alone of any one member country, decided a few years ago that they wanted to swap certain activities so that each would become more competitive in a more defined area, it would have been quite impossible for any national jurisdiction to control effectively the impact of that swap. It rapidly became clear, on investigation, that there were problems, and these were specifically related to the carpet-fibre sector, where the two companies had been in competition between themselves, and where this competition had kept wholesale prices down because of the competition. Now, that competition was to be eliminated by the swap: and carpet manufacturers and supplies needed to be reassured that they would not be faced with a single monopoly supplier, able to raise wholesale prices, and by extension consumer prices, at will. In practice, the Commission, acting on behalf of the EU, was able to take the right precautions, and ensured that when the swap went through, there were the right safety clauses included to ensure that smaller supplier or purchaser companies did not find themselves rapidly forced out of the market.

In a similar case, the giant food group Nestlé wanted to buy Perrier – you may remember that Perrier got into trouble after minute quantities of Benzene were found in its distinctive green bottles, and that as result its world sales fell off dramatically. Here, the issues were rather different – mineral waters are a very different market to carpet fibres, but in France, for example, they are a cut-throat market. If Nestlé had been allowed to buy Perrier without selling off any of its other mineral water brands, it would have had rather more of the market than would be good for the consumer – so the conclusion imposed by the Commission was that it could take over Perrier, but only if it disposed of a range of other brands sufficient to bring its overall share of the market down to a reasonable level.

I will not go into more detail about competition law, but I would like to stress the general point about bringing prices down. Many EU policies have this effect, not just anti-trust laws. I have already mentioned action against monopolies, for example, and the introduction of competition into many markets which have traditionally been regarded as public service markets. Opening up national monopolies in telecommunications is forcing prices down, providing greater choice to the benefit of both individuals and industry.

Similarly, in the transport field, the EU has liberalised airline traffic and prices. It has introduced competition into a wide variety of routes, even where the countries concerned did not necessarily want it. You may have seen in the press that the Commission obliged the French government to open three routes from Paris's second airport at Orly – to London, to Marseille and to Toulouse – to airlines other than the state-owned Air Inter. The first complainant in this affair was TAT – a French subsidiary of British Airways. But it should be said that once the French government had given in, the first airlines to benefit from the opening were not in fact TAT, they were Air Liberté and Air Littoral, two small French companies which had been excluded by their own government from these lucrative routes, and needed the weight of the EU to get in. The result is already visible: Air Inter has slashed its fares for the routes concerned, as a result of which it has been matched by all the other airlines involved; consumers have a wider choice of airlines from which to choose, and they have better prices than they had before.

Finally, I would like to cite another way in which the individual stands to benefit from the EU – and here, I feel that I am on home ground with you tonight.

The EU spends an enormous amount on research and the circulation and dissemination of information and experience. It encourages collaborative projects and the sharing of expertise, across a vast range of subjects. This may be in the Research and Development field, where the EU's Fourth Framework Research programme will provide over 13 billion ECUs, or £10 billion during five years; it may be through programmes such as ERASMUS, COMETT and TEMPUS – soon to be subsumed within SOCRATES – which provide for student and teacher exchange and partnership within the EU and beyond its borders and for which £600 million has been earmarked: or it may be through campaigns of public awareness, such as the Europe against cancer campaign. None of these activities is constraining upon member countries, upon companies, universities and colleges, or upon individuals. In fields such as these, the EU has nothing to harmonise or lay down. But it is very proper for the EU to set up what I might call opt-in programmes – to give those who want to take part in European collaboration, for whom the exercise can be exciting and professionally rewarding, a chance to do so. And behind the researcher, the lecturer, the student or the health worker lies the mass of individual citizens, for whose benefit all these activities, in the long term are carried on. Thousands of students and academics have had their horizons widened and their job prospects enlarged by being given the opportunity to study or teach elsewhere in the EU as a result of the EU programmes.

THE FUTURE

The debate over whether the EU is valuable to the individual, and in what ways, will continue. It forms a backdrop to the debate we shall have as the EU prepares for the next Inter-Governmental Conference, due in 1996, at which the Treaties will be looked at again and changes brought in to respond to our current needs. Some trends though, have already become clear over recent years.

The first is a trend to reduce the amount of legislation coming out of Brussels. This is not something that can usefully be calcu-lated by adding up draft directives and working out the trend – though if you do that, you will find that it is downward – but rather a matter of the types of law which the EU now makes.

There was a big surge of legislation involved in setting up the Internal Market. That has now largely been completed, and we no longer have that mass of legislation to get though. We should now be aiming for what I might call less but better – for less legislation, but for it to be in areas where there is clear added value from joint action at EU level, over and above what member countries individually can achieve.

In that context, I believe that individual rights will grow, not diminish. I have already spoken of the Barber judgement, which was a response by the Court to a claim from an individual. The European Court of Justice has also held that under certain circumstances, directives can create individual rights for the citizen, and that these can be asserted in law against a government which has not transposed EU legislation properly, or indeed not at all. In these cases, for which there are obviously specific criteria that have to be fulfiled, an individual or a company may have a claim for compensation against a government which has not fulfiled its duties under EU law. The same is also true in a wide range of Community matters, where EU decisions or legislation can give rise to rights under civil law. Indeed, I sometimes wonder why more companies do not seek remedies under EU law through national courts. When I was responsible in the Commission for Competition policy, I persuaded my colleagues to agree to a public notice to encourage the use by potential complainants of national courts, with the twin aims of ensuring speedier justice, and, I have to admit, of reducing the numbers who looked to the Commission for relief. This is one way in which the individual can enforce his rights, and people should be encouraged to use it to the full.

Indeed, the EU's Court is sensitive to individual rights. It is now many years since it began to rule that the basic human rights accepted in Europe – and, in particular, as set out in the European Charter of Human Rights – formed part of the legal heritage of member states; and that the European Community Treaties had therefore to be interpreted in a way which was consistent with those rights. Although human rights do not figure directly in the treaties, it is clear that the Court regards them as an essential back cloth to its work, and that interpretations of the treaties which go against them would be avoided at all costs.

I believe also that further individual rights, similar to those which have been defended by the Court so far, would not be out of place. I have myself proposed a new Article 119 A of the Treaty, outlawing racial discrimination at work on exactly the same basis as Art 119 itself does for discrimination between men and women. This would not be difficult to introduce – the jurisprudence of the Court on Equal Opportunities is such as to enable its implementation to be rapid and effective. You may ask – why should this be limited to outlawing discrimination at work? Is not racism a hydra which needs slaying wherever it rears one of its heads? The answer is that yes it does – but the EU only has limited powers, and while it must act effectively when it does act, it must stay within the limits they imply. The EU does have competence for work-related matters – but not, say, for housing, for social security, or for any of the host of other areas where racial discrimination can, and does, rear up its ugly head.

My suggestion in this field has been well received. I believe that it would represent a significant advance for the EU – a demonstration that it can respond to changes in circumstances since its foundation treaties were drafted, and that it does have the capacity to respond to the desires of a large and growing number of its citizens. I hope that governments will have the vision to take up this change when they come to look at the Treaty again in 1996.

I believe that the single other way in which governments could make the individual more interested in, and more appreciative of the EU would be to increase the degree of transparency in the way it works and to ensure that it does limit itself strictly to doing what is better done at EU level – practising, and not just preaching, subsidiarity.

So far as transparency is concerned, there are many steps that could be taken, particularly in the education system. Obviously, schoolchildren learn about how British government works, but they should surely also learn about how the EU works as well – as part of their civic education. It would take time for that to filter through to the population at large, but it would be a good start to know that even that was happening.

Subsidiarity, however, is another matter. It produces very mixed reactions at EU level – some member states take it very seriously, such as Britain or Germany; others regard it all as a plot to renationalise matters currently dealt with at EU level. In practice, it is a common sense principle. Decisions should be taken at a level as close as possible to the individual affected by them. The EU should be brought in only where there is added value in its doing so – where we can achieve more acting together, than we can by adding up the capacities of our component member countries. Where this is the case, then let the EU come in – and let it act efficiently, rapidly, and in a way which responds to what its citizens need and want. But where there is no added value, the EU should keep out, leaving Women's Institute Jams on the village market place and freshwater shellfish on their river beds, not regulating the sale of pure-bred horses or dogs or the use of knocking copy in advertising, and understanding that levels of blood-alcohol in drunken drivers are definitely best left to individual member countries to set. In none of these areas is there real added value in common legislation – so in none of them should the EU act. Learning this lesson is essential in all the EU's institutions – including both the European Parliment and the Council of Ministers, where governments are as guilty as the Commission of making legislation far too precise, and of building in unnecessary frills round the edges to satisfy one or other constituency, which may look negligible individually, but taken all together make the legislation far more constraining and rigid than is desirable.

CONCLUSION

It is no accident that a fair analysis of what the EU has actually done over the years shows that it has promoted both the interests and the welfare of Europeans as individuals. This is no accident, because a belief in the primacy of the individual is one of the distinctive values underlying the diverse cultures which together make up the European Union. These diverse cultures must not and will not be submerged in some vague and amorphous European entity. Quite the reverse. The European Union can enhance and strengthen the various cultures represented within it. But there are certain values that we share in common.

For example when town-twinning celebrations lead to exchanges of firemen, small business men or school children, they do find something in common. And that something is an understanding that the individual lies at the heart of society _ that our systems of welfare, of health care of education, of justice, of democracy are designed for the benefit of the individual and not to enable him to serve some all-encompassing state. I believe that this fundamental truth lies as much at the heart of the EU as it does at the heart of its member countries. It is why only genuinely democratic states can expect admission to the EU, and why the countries wanting to join the EU, whether in Eastern Europe or elsewhere, have to demonstrate, as they are doing, that democracy has taken deep root within them, and is secure and flourishing. It is also why over time, the individual's rights in the EU will continue to strengthen, to be entrenched by legislation and by the Courts. It is why the passage of time is indeed a passage 'Towards a Europe for the Individual'.

Printed in the United States
By Bookmasters